Stefano Caprio

# The mystique of the new Rome

Stefano Caprio

# The mystique of the new Rome

ScienciaScripts

**Imprint**
Any brand names and product names mentioned in this book are subject to trademark, brand or patent protection and are trademarks or registered trademarks of their respective holders. The use of brand names, product names, common names, trade names, product descriptions etc. even without a particular marking in this work is in no way to be construed to mean that such names may be regarded as unrestricted in respect of trademark and brand protection legislation and could thus be used by anyone.

Cover image: www.ingimage.com

This book is a translation from the original published under ISBN 978-620-2-06899-4.

Publisher:
Sciencia Scripts
is a trademark of
Dodo Books Indian Ocean Ltd. and OmniScriptum S.R.L publishing group

120 High Road, East Finchley, London, N2 9ED, United Kingdom
Str. Armeneasca 28/1, office 1, Chisinau MD-2012, Republic of Moldova, Europe
Printed at: see last page
**ISBN: 978-620-8-23439-3**

## Table of contents

## CHAPTER 1

## THE TALE OF SVETOMIR THE PRINCE: MYTH AND THEOLOGICAL THOUGHT.

*Stefano Caprio, 04.05.2016 - Pontifical Oriental Institute*

It is not easy to define the work and personality of such a multifaceted and versatile author as Vyacheslav Ivanov, who lived at the turn of two centuries and great changes in his country and in the world, so deeply connected to his land, and yet so genetically aspiring to the spheres of the wider and universal, as the very theme of the international conference at the Pontifical Oriental Institute, *Dialectics of the universal / temporal (historical) in Vyacheslav Ivanov and his contemporaries*, not coincidentally testifies. A master of the Russian word and a polyglot like few others, the founder of the philosophically grounded Symbolist movement, capable at the same time of distancing himself from the Symbolists in the name of absolute realism, a religious thinker on the borderline between scholastic dogmatics and mythological syncretism, a Russian European of which there are few, a proponent of the spiritual unity of Christian faiths of East and West, ancient and modern cultures, the most diverse genres of art and expression, Vyacheslav "the Magnificent", as Gershenzon called him in *Correspondence from Two Corners*, may seem to some as a misunderstood genius, to others as an unfinished talent, or as an unheard prophet who still holds many secrets.

The intellectual life of the Russian poet and thinker had many roads travelled and turning points. A pupil of Vladimir Soloviev, in his youthful years he seemed eager to assimilate the totality of humanistic knowledge by studying the past under Theodor Mommsen, "the greatest master of historical exposition," as stated in the justification for the Nobel Prize awarded to him for his History of Rome, which was of great importance to Ivanov himself. His studies of Greek and Roman antiquity are probably his most valuable legacy, for Ivanov did not limit himself to commentary and explanation, but by penetrating as one of the protagonists inside an archaic symbol or myth, he was able to show universal, transversal and ever-new dimensions and spaces. Ivanov did not try to preserve or improve the ancient and noble remains of irretrievably lost times, but on his own initiative took their forms and energies, discovering that under the mask of power, religion and politics, culture and war, angels and demons, from the creation of the world and even earlier, there are spaces of the soul that interact with the destinies of people, nations and gods.

Born into the Orthodox faith, he spent his entire life in an incessant search for the truth of other faiths, until his solemn entry into the Roman Church proclaimed the supreme truth of the universal and therefore "catholic" faith, capable of saving, purifying and perfecting every spiritual aspiration, of completing the process of maturing the inner organism of man and the world, of breathing "with both lungs," as he put it in the ecumenical formula that gained worldwide recognition. Ivanov was a contemporary of religious eclecticism, which from its Gnostic and Masonic roots produced Feuerbach's "devout atheism" and Marxist eschatology, Dostoevsky's existential Christomonism and Nietzschean mystical theory of the superman, up to Tolstoy's populist pacifism, perhaps the most widespread religion today in its many directions and new formulations.

The religious-historical quest of the late nineteenth century was provoked by a radical critique of religion and Christianity, originating from the evolution of Illuminist philosophy and from Hegelian historicism itself. This criticism was carried to extreme expression by Feuerbach in The *Essence of Christianity* of 1841, and finally by Nietzsche's fierce denunciation in *Antichrist*, written at the end of the century. This was the precondition for the militant atheism of subsequent regimes, for the resolute anti-clerical struggle of the dominant ideologies in Europe and in the world. Christianity, seen as the decay of the true human spirit, was presented as the main enemy to be destroyed, as a brake on moral and intellectual progress, a justification for the oppressive regimes of the past. The most acute challenge found its formulation in Friedrich Nietzsche's initial reflection on the *Birth of Tragedy,* conceived in the "Wagnerian" phase of the 1970s and repeatedly returned to in the following years, up to and including the cry of *Merry Science* proclaiming "the death of God." In the Nietzschean reading of Greek culture, the victory of Apollonian "moralism" over "Dionysian" creativity became the fundamental category for the indictment of Christianity, guilty of internalising the dictatorship of religious law over the human spirit. The philosopher himself declared that the aim of his critique of Greek antiquity was precisely this:

*"Perhaps the full depth of this anti-moral inclination can be gauged by the diligent and hostile silence with which Christianity is treated in this book - Christianity as the most unmeasured, polyphonic presentation of the moral theme that mankind has ever heard..... From the very beginning, essentially and fundamentally, Christianity was fatigue and disgust - experienced by life from life itself, and only covered, and hidden, and dressed up by the belief in a "different" or "better" life .*[1]

[1] Friedrich Nietzsche, *La nascita della tragedia, ovvero grecita e pessimismo,* ed. italiana a cura di Paolo Chiarini con la collaborazione di Roberto Venuti, Laterza, Bari 2012 (7th ed.), p.11.

The overcoming of Christianity, according to Nietzsche, lay in a return to the true potentialities of human nature, in that aesthetic intuition which would lead ultimately to the theory of *Ubermensch'.*

*"So then, with all the dubious questioning of this book, my instinct, the advocate of life, turned against morality, then it composed for itself its principled counter-teaching, its counter-evaluation of life: purely artistic, anti-Christian. What should we call it? Being a philologist, a man of words, I am not without a certain liberty - for who knows the real name of the Antichrist? - I christened him in the name of a Greek god: I called him Dionysian " .* [2]

In the Dionysian expression of the human will, art is the true dimension of its search for realisation and self-awareness, where one relies more on the risk of self-transcendence than on ethical and religious answers:

"The Dionysian ... *is that colossal horror which seizes man when he suddenly happens to doubt the forms of knowledge of phenomena, because, as it seems to him, the law of sufficient reason begins to undergo an exception in one of its guises. If to the horror we add also the bliss of rapture, rising from the innermost foundation of man and even of the whole nature at the sight of the same destruction of the principium individuationis, then by doing so we will cast a glance inside the essence of the Dionysian, the closest analogy of which is a hangover. Either under the influence of narcotic drinking, about which all primitive people and nations speak in hymns, or with spring, the mighty proximity of which permeates all nature with its joys, the Dionysian movements of the soul awaken, and with their increase the subjective gradually melts away, reaching the fullest self-forgetfulness.... It is unwise to turn away from such phenomena as if from epidemics in the consciousness of one's own health - by doing so, they make it clear: they are "healthy", the Muses sitting on the edge of the forest with Dionysus in the middle escape into the thicket, or even in the waves of the sea, as soon as such a "Master of the Basis" suddenly appears before them"*[3] .

We have turned to these fiery words of Nietzsche, dating back to Ivanov's childhood years, because they became for the Russian poet an epochal challenge to which he devoted his life and his intellectual energies. As he himself writes in his 1917 *Autobiographical Letter* to Vengerov, in his adolescence he experienced a crisis of faith during which

*"It is noteworthy that my love for Christ and dreams of Him did not fade away,*

---

[2] *Ibid,* p. 12.
[3] Ibid., p.25.

*but even flared up during the period of my godlessness. He was also the protagonist of my first poems..... Passion for Dostoevsky fuelled this mystical attraction, which I sought to reconcile with the philosophical denial of religion"*[4] .

Ivanov emerged from his youthful crisis with a mission in life that consisted precisely in the "reconciliation" of spirit and reason. He grasped the deep foundations of the Nietzschean critique, which was so prophetic that even today it still leaves its imprint on the general consciousness of the religious phenomenon: faith must not stifle freedom, modern man can no longer accept the moralistic denigration of religious feeling. A passionate love for Christ, further fuelled by doubts and philosophical criticism, suggested to Ivanov a new manifestation of Christianity, not contrary to tradition or official theology, but still capable of combining nihilist tendencies with the recognition of the presence of the divine, moreover with its very incarnation.

After studying and researching classical antiquity, Ivanov set about describing the *Hellenic religion of the suffering god, the* formula through which he wanted to find a link between Hellenic paganism and Christianity. Ivanov's attempt to turn Nietzschean rage into a positive is completely original: the "religion of Dionysus," conceived by the Prussian philosopher as an archetype of anti-Christianity, becomes for Ivanov a prophecy of a Christianity more authentic and catholic, universal and humanistic. In 1903 Ivanov gave a course of lectures in Paris on the religious cult of Dionysus, publishing then essays on *".the Hellenic religion of the suffering god"* in 1904 and on *"The Religion of Dionysus"* in 1905, thus coming to write in 1921 his doctoral thesis *"Dionysus and Pradionysianism",* which was published in Baku in 1923. Thus the Dionysian theme runs through the whole period of success and tragedy, from the literary and philosophical circles that earned the name of the "Silver Age" and generated a whirlwind of poetic, philosophical and religious creativity that had few equals in the history of the spirit until the apocalyptic revolution of 1917, man's most serious attempt to redraw God and every form of worship of Him.

Ivanov carried this extraordinary baggage and this bleeding wound with him into his voluntary Roman exile, where he not only distanced himself from revolutionary Russia but also distanced himself from the entire Russian artistic and cultural world, at home or in exile. Despite open communication with all those who wanted answers from him to the agonising questions of those terrible and startling years, he lived for a quarter of a century in Italy, first in Pavia and then in Rome, in another "tower" of the spirit, in which it was the spirit of Dionysus that lifted him where only a few could reach him. Ivanov, as the historical mentor of Russian spiritualism, did not attempt to combat

---

[4]See Shishkin, A., A *Brief Chronicle of the Life and Work of Vyacheslav Ivanov*, at v-ivanov.it.

Soviet atheism by counter-propaganda, nor did he support the attempts of his friends in Paris, Berlin, or America to keep the flag of the Russian soul in exile; after his adoption of Catholicism, he was by no means involved in Roman Catholic projects for the "conquest" of Russia, as the great strategist d'Herbigny had suggested to him. His way out of the darkness of atheistic nihilism could not be divided; it passed from mythological transfiguration, from the application of lost symbols to that reality which was to be completely reborn. It was from these feelings that his great idea was born and gradually developed: to merge ancient mythology with the Russian soul, to express in archaic form the need for a new life, to cross literary styles and genres in order to give birth to a new model of universal Christianity. And this idea was realised in the epic form of the *Tale of Svetomir the Tsarevich.*

The poem is the last work of Vyacheslav Ivanov, to which he devoted himself mainly during the Italian period of his life, beginning in 1928 and, most of all, during the fifteen years (1936-1949) of his final stay in Rome, until his death, which came on 16 July 1949 in his flat on the Aventine. The sense that this was a prophetic work is reinforced by the fact that a petition was presented to Pope Pius XI to fund the philosopher's work in order to allow him to complete his last great work. In the petition to the Pope, the then Rector of the Russicum, Fr. De Régis explained that

*"He [Ivanov] wished to publish a work in which, under the guise of a story or a novel, he would express his whole conception of life and religion, and which would be a spiritual testament originating from his autobiography. This work would have had a great resonance in the history of Russian thought and would have been linked to Vladimir Soloviev's book* Russia and the Universal Church".

Pius XI approved the granting of the regular salary allocated to Ivanov as a lecturer at the Russicum and the Pontifical Oriental Institute, allowing him to not worry about material needs and to complete his ambitious vision. The motivation for De Régis's petition is explanatory: Soloviev attempted to interpret the history of Christianity and the history of Russia, deducing from this a kind of programme of "free theocracy", combining the thoroughness of the Roman primacy with Russian sobornost, a communion experienced in freedom. His adoption of Catholicism, which inspired Ivanov's similar decision, expressed the meaning of this synthesis; the disciple, in turn, fifty years later wanted to try to present the path of universal unity that would allow the "Dionysian" power of the Russian soul to be unleashed on the granite foundation of the "Apollonian" Catholicism of Rome.

Soloviev's attempt faded, unheeded by either the Church of the East or the West, even if Pope Leo XIII expressed his approval of the Russian philosopher's intentions, and may have drawn inspiration from them in formulating the foundations of the Catholic Church's social teaching. Soloviev's desire for Christian unity was thus elevated in the final apocalyptic vision of the famous *Legend of the Antichrist*, where the surviving representatives of the churches resist the globalising charms of a false universal religion. Paying tribute to his teacher, Vyacheslav Ivanov decided to turn to the form of "legend" in his *Tale*, which is also a rather unusual literary form, as the author himself admits in his letter to the translator Von Geiseler: "The novel-legend, both in form and content, is something completely new, stylised after the Middle Ages and hagiographies of saints.... I wanted to convey an aged style of narration, which also includes a certain number of mystical songs in the folk manner"[5] . The aim of this was to recreate the power of the Dionysian myth, but in a form that unites the Russian epic with the sacred story, a transversal language that expresses "the boundary between the man-made and the non-man-made", as S. Averintsev says. Averintsev in his preface to the edition of Ivanov's works, "the cathedral soul of the world is ontologically lower than the Creator, but higher than all the private forces detached from the unity of individuals, which these souls harass as false bridegrooms, beginning with the fallen angels." It was Averintsev, Ivanov's true heir, who understood the spirit of Ivanov's legend, which consists in rewriting the cosmogonic and soteriological myths of Hellenism through a completely original prism of the Russian soul.

In fact, Ivanov's work fits into a large-scale literary and philosophical trend of the late nineteenth and early twentieth centuries, beginning with Nietzsche proper with his *Also sprach Zarathustra*, where he attempted to express profound philosophical and spiritual concepts in fantastic and narrative form by appealing to Greek and Persian religious mythology. A more general frame of reference is undoubtedly the Wagnerian cycle *The Ring of the Nibelung, which* inspired the legendary stories of Tolkien*'s Lord of the Rings and* Lewis*'s Chronicles of Narnia*, as well as Thomas Mann's biblical reading of *Joseph and His Brothers,* authors related to Ivanov not only by temporal proximity but also by pedagogical and narrative sensitivity. Ivanov's characters, however, are overt stylisations of the epic heroes of Russian history, the ancient chronicles and its bylinas. This is how the Tale begins, recalling the events of ancient Kievan Rus:

1,1;1-7

1 *The tale of Svetomir the Tsarevich, son of Vladyar the Tsar, begins:*

2 *In the white kingdom, the Christian state, King Volodar held sway.*

[5] *Letter to the translator von Geiseler*, 1930.

*3 In his hand the dominion was established and magnified, and his dominion extended to the east of the sun and noon and west and midnight afar off, and his name filled the universe;*

*4 and the people worked for the power, and the land bore the burdens of the kingdom.*

*5 And the sovereign Volodar sat down in a great ruin and devastation, and defended his homeland from the oppressors, and soon he raised it to greater glory,*

*6 He did not inherit his father's table, but was favoured and shown and planted by the grace of God, by the blessing of the church and by the will of the whole earth,*

*7 at the signs revealed from Saint Egoriy, as a risen leader in the power of Egoriy, from the root of the Lord's Warrior; and the earth was not ashamed of the hope.*

*8 And before that the life of Volodarev was as follows.*

It also mentions conflicts between ancient principalities and the uncertain beginning of the establishment of Christianity in the Russian lands:

1, П, 1-2

*1 The memory is alive in the world: Egorius the Brave had six forest sisters, and their natural brother enlightened them with the light of Christ in the darkness of ignorance.*

*2 Their sons and grandsons, more than the maternal instruction of their fathers and grandfathers, committed themselves to wickedness and enchantment, and apostatised from the holy faith, except for one confessor of Christ, and that one was martyred in his youthful years, were possessed by fratricidal rage, and in the internecine strife of one another they did not eradicate one another.*

In this legendary-historical context, the theological-mythical cycle of Svetomir develops, which takes a cataphatic and uncovering path through the stages of death and resurrection, revolution and restoration of the natural order, always around the identity of the tsarevitch and his female soul, embodied in the figure of the female mother-daughter-saint and finally in the fusion of the masculine and feminine. The whole poem is built around the triple figure of the father Lazarus, who is transformed into Vladyar and finally gives birth to his son Svetomir, in the trinitarian allegory of Father-Spirit and Son, accompanied by the superimposition of two female figures (Solovyev's Sophia) Gorislava and Otrada, and finally in the synthesis of Svetomir the Tsar/Maiden himself. The supreme example of Ivanov's reworking of the Paschal and Baptismal mystery is the death of Gorislava, who gives birth to Otrada at the "Egor's Key", which recalls the Baptism of Rus' in the Dnieper:

I, XIX

1 *Gorislava went to Egor's Key and prayed at the cross above the krinitsa.*

2 *And when she prayed, she felt that her hour was coming, and she embraced the cross with her hands, kneeling on her knees; and the pains of labour seized her, but she did not let go of the cross from her hands, and as she grasped it, she held on more and more tightly, until after a short agony she was released from the burden.*

3 *And, having given birth to a daughter, she rose from the cross through great strength, and washed the child with water from the cemetery, and having lifted up exorbitant labour, and not looking at the fatigue of death, she carried the newborn child to Vasilisa and laid it in her arms,*

4 *She herself went to bed, her body exhausted to the point of exhaustion, but her soul was resurrected. And, lightly rejoicing, she said, overcoming the exhaustion of the flesh, about the child: "My joy is born.*

5 *And they called the daughter of Simeon and Gorislava in holy baptism Euphrosinia, which means: joy; and they always called her Otrada.*

6 *And when Joy was baptised, a peaceful angel came to Gorislava's bedside and took her soul out of her mouth.*

7 *Joy was born under the Apple Saviour, and under the Dormition Day they buried Gorislava; and they laid her, according to her mortification, in the reserved oak-tree of Egor'eva.*

The new birth of the eternally feminine, Sophia, who revives the image of God in man, is close to the mystical visions of Vladimir Soloviev; in Vyacheslav Ivanov's "legend" it becomes a new prophecy of life and resurrection. Overcoming "mortal fatigue", a phenomenon more characteristic than ever of modernity, the poet calls for the proclamation of the joy of a newfound identity, of the union of the human with the divine, of the small nature of the individual with the universal communion of heavenly forces.

Ivanov is thus not only the exponent of a splendid synthesis of the numerous tendencies of Russian Symbolism of the Silver Age. He can quite deservedly be classified among the narrow circle of "Russian theologians," that amazing group of thinkers and visionaries who drew from the very special contamination of genres typical of the Russian soul the inspiration for a new reading of the entire Christian teaching. Solov'ev was the first, after attempting to penetrate the "locked garden" of Russian academic theology at the Moscow Academy, to address the whole of Russia, travelling to St. Petersburg, the city of the ambiguous eschatological destiny of the empire, and producing those startling *Readings on the God-Man* (1877-1881) which so shocked the old prophet Dostoevsky that he used Solov'ev as the prototype of his last messenger, the "monk in the world," Alyosha Karamazov. In his *Readings, the* young philosopher resolutely takes up the theological tradition of the first councils and its untouchable definitions, in particular the union of Christ's two natures proclaimed at Chalcedon, in order to formulate his vision of Christological universalism, thus bringing to a close the Slavophile reflection on Schelling*'s Alleinheit*. According to Solovyov, there are two types of unity in every organism, the active, unity of Theandria, which is the creation of the Logos, the One who draws to himself, and the passive, feminine type of Sophia, the reflection of divinity in the relativity of matter. This organism is accomplished in history through a process of union that creates the Church, "Humanity, reunited with its divine beginning through the mediation of Jesus Christ" (Reading 11). These are the principles of sophiology, that attempt at synthesis by which the Russians endeavoured to express for modernity the great truths of holy Christianity.

Solovyov's disciples, in turn, tried in different directions to offer new interpretations of Sophia theology. Pavel Florensky chose to focus on the first of the great councils, the Council of Nicaea, that is, the trinitarian dogma rather than the Christological dogma, in his Orthodox theodicy The *Pillar and Affirmation of Truth* (1913), to describe lived religious experience, "the only legitimate way of knowing the dogmas," emphasising the three-dimensional analogies of space, time, and man in the epistemology of the Triune Subject's self-proving from the Nicene homoousia. Sergius Bulgakov, for his part, attempted to re-read the dogma of the Second Council of Nicaea on the Christology of the icon, revising the theological arguments of the iconoclasts.

His study The *Icon and Iconoclasm,* published in Paris in 1930, but conceived in earlier studies on the icon, grasps the aporia of the dogmatic definitions themselves, which do not provide sufficient grounds for the original aniconicity of Christianity; the true image of God is man and the whole world in which the revelation of divine Sophia takes place, that special "harmonisation of the human and the divine" about which the Catholic theologian Hans Urs von Balthasar, who not coincidentally was also indebted to Solov'ev's thought, would reflect extensively in the twentieth century. To this Russian thirst to rediscover Christianity we can refer the existentialism of Berdyaev and Shestov, the intuitionism of Nikolai Lossky and Semyon Frank, or the philosophy of spiritual experience of Ivan Ilyin. Such was also the mad intuition of the couple who founded Symbolism, the "new church of the holy spirit" of Dmitri Merezhkovsky and Zinaida Gippius, and in some ways the dream of spiritual revolution of Blok, Beloi, and many other companions of Vyacheslav Ivanov.

In the *Tale of Svetomir the Prince* he even tried to bring back into the mainstream of the great dogmatic tradition its chief and mortal enemy, ancient Hellenic Gnosticism: in the new version of the Valentinian myth, the Aeons of Ivan disintegrate and reunite in order to regain the unity of the divine being, and the image of Gorislava embracing the cross is a direct reference to the fallen Sophia finding her wholeness in union with Christ. The ancient Gnostics, the creative heirs of Greek mythology, were the first to make a bold attempt to convey the Gospel revelation by the means of classical culture, and from this was practically born the whole of holy theology, in its Alexandrian version and in its Antiochian counterpoint. If in the third century, the most learned man was the Neoplatonist Origen, and in the Middle Ages the synthesis took place thanks to the Aristotelian logic of Thomas and the mythopoetic theory of Dante, the new theology of modern times found in such great scholars as Solovyov and Ivanov a new light, the "evening of the beyond" of the incessantly fulfilling new creation, the call not to imprison oneself in formulas, living faith, which is man's free response to the divine vocation.

## CHAPTER 2

## At the origins of modern spiritualism: the legacy of Nietzsche

The religiosity of the twenty-first century is undoubtedly astonishing, and hardly fits into any rigid scheme, given the crisis of the great traditional religions, the emergence of new religious communities and movements, and the fact that the great enlightenment and positivist critique of religion during the modern era has exhausted itself. Without going into a discussion of the definition of what is postmodern, let us turn rather to the prophetic period of religious philosophy at the turn of the nineteenth and twentieth centuries, which only now, as it seems to us, is showing us its fruits. The challenge posed to religions by the so-called "maestros of suspicion" of the late nineteenth century led numerous Christian thinkers to seek new categories of understanding of the supernatural and openness to divine revelation. Stifled by the confrontations and bloc divisions of the twentieth century, today these reflections are re-emerging in a rather unstable and obscure context, including and above all from a religious point of view.

This period, in the context of the great European discussion of the early twentieth century in Russia, is labelled the "silver age", thus indicating one of the pinnacles of the country's cultural history, in comparison with the most celebrated "golden age" of the nineteenth century. The key to the continuity between these two periods is the work of various writers and thinkers whose work crosses the boundary of these two phases, such as the two greatest representatives of Russian literature, Fyodor Dostoevsky and Leo Tolstoy. It was during the "Silver Age" that a distinctly spiritualist tendency, also called "Russian religious philosophy", was established, one of the prominent representatives of which can rightly be considered the Russian symbolist poet Vyacheslav Ivanov. This text is dedicated to him.

The very definition of "religious philosophy" goes back to the great German philosopher Friedrich Schelling, who tried to summarise the results of his metaphysics of nature in the philosophy of religion. In Russia, Schelling's ideas took on a new life as part of a more general debate about the historical destiny of Russian culture, which in the nineteenth century saw a confrontation between Schellingian Slavophiles and Westerners who referred more to Hegel's ideas. One of the founding fathers of Slavophilism, the philosopher Ivan Kireyevsky, a direct disciple of Schelling, pointed out a path to follow, a programme of religious philosophy necessary not only for Russia but for the whole of universal culture. We find his fundamental ideas in a kind of spiritual testament of the philosopher entitled *On the Necessity and Possibility of New Beginnings for Philosophy*, where Kireyevsky tries to outline the directions of the "new" Christian philosophy, motivated by the need to overcome Aristotelian rationalism introduced by scholasticism: "How could the Roman Church break away otherwise from the Church of the Universe? She fell away from it only because she wanted to introduce into the faith new dogmas unknown to the Church's tradition and generated by the accidental conclusion of the logic of the Western nations. Hence occurred that first bifurcation in the very basic beginning of Western doctrine, out of which developed first scholastic philosophy within the faith, then reformation in the faith, and finally philosophy outside the faith. The first rationalists were scholastics; their offspring are called Hegelians." In Kireyevsky's opinion, an arbitrary reading of the ancient classics of antiquity has led modern theologians astray: "The basic convictions of Aristotle - not those attributed to him by his medieval interpreters, but those that come out of his writings - are absolutely identical with those of Hegel."

Thus, according to the Slavophile philosopher, it is necessary to proceed from a correct understanding of Greek thought, to which the great fathers of the Church turned, and the consequences of which are still evident in the history of Christian culture: "Ancient Greek philosophy also arose not directly from Greek beliefs, but by their influence and under them, arose from their inner disagreement. The inner discord of the faith compelled an abstract reasonableness. Thus with the final development of Greek education ended, we may say, the dominion of pagan beliefs over the enlightenment of mankind; not because there were no more believing pagans left, but because the advanced thought of education was already outside the pagan faith, turning mythology into allegory.... From this negative side Greek philosophy appears in the life of mankind as a useful educator of the mind (...). Philosophy prepared the field for Christian sowing".

Kireyevsky recalls the long struggle waged by Christian thinkers against the falsity of pagan mythology, and the Aristotelian rationalism that was its consequence, in order to arrive at that "Christian wisdom" which produced the dogmas of the first councils. A return to the teachings of the Church Fathers was in fact one of the basic principles that inspired Slavophilism, in particular Kireyevsky himself, who drew closer to the monastic worlds precisely in order to return to these ancient roots. In his view, the break with ancient wisdom was caused by the ignorance into which the Western world had fallen during the early Middle Ages, once again mired in the contradictions of paganism. A striking example of this, taken from the classic polemic between Orthodoxy and the Catholics, was the introduction of the Filioque into the Creed, which Kireyevsky called "the first triumph of rationalism over faith": in order to confront the Arian heritage, the Western Church ignorantly chose a formulation directly opposed to Arianism, forgetting that truth is not derived from the direct opposite of error, but by virtue of some inherent expressiveness. The tragic result of this delusion, according to the philosopher, was the stoppage of the development of Christian thought not only in the West, but also in the East: "What should have been accomplished by the combined efforts of the East and the West was no longer possible for the East alone, which was thus doomed only to preserve the divine truth in its purity and holiness, without being able to embody it in the external education of the peoples".

Thus, the Slavophile reading focuses on the need for a "new beginning", and at the same time a return to the origins and a new formulation of Christian truth, entrusted to a "new people" capable of making the heritage of the Christian East fruitful again, and of understanding and correcting the errors of the West: "Who knows? Perhaps this outward impotence of the East was destined to continue until the age when another people, enlightened by true Christianity at the very time when the West was falling away from the East, would grow and mature in place of the fallen Rome; It may be that this new nation is destined to come to mental maturity at the very time when the enlightenment of the West, by the power of its own development, will destroy the force of its foreign teaching and will pass from false beliefs in Christianity to indifferent philosophical beliefs, returning the world to the times of pre-Christian thinking."

Consequently, Russian Orthodoxy in the Slavophile conception is much more than just another offering of ancient tradition; it is a new synthesis of East and West, a new proclamation of Christianity to modern thought, dried up and secularised by centuries of scholastic rationalism. The task set by Kireyevsky was enthusiastically embraced by the whole Russian philosophical thought of the nineteenth century, and in a sense, even if in a completely opposite way, by the opposing side, that is, by the Westerners: The revolutionary and palingenetic excitement, which from the Hegelianism of Herzen and Belinsky passed on to the nihilism of Bakunin and the radicalism of Chernyshevsky, right up to the movements that would lead to the events of the twentieth century, also responds to the desire to remake the world and to teach a new truth about it. The co-founder of the Slavophile movement, the publicist Alexei Khomyakov, realised Kireyevsky's philosophical insights in a new theory about the essence of Christianity and the nature of the Christian Church, known as the doctrine of *Sobornost*, or the mystical unity of men by the power of the Holy Spirit, which, although never officially adopted by the Orthodox Church, has always been appealed to by all the most eminent thinkers and the hierarchy itself. The puzzling revelation of the *Russian Christ* in the novels of Fyodor Dostoevsky is precisely an attempt to discover a new way of faith, a higher and more paradoxical truth of human reason, while the great moralist Tolstoy, atheist and Westerner, was attempting in the foundation of the path of Christian humanistic spirituality.

The most truly Russian of the writers of the rapid manifestation of Slavophilism, Nikolai Gogol, expressed the ideas of Kirievsky in one letter to the great poet Zhukovsky, announcing to him that the time had come for the Russian Orthodox Church and the realisation of its great mission in history: "There is a reconciler of everything within our land itself, which is not yet seen by everyone - our Church. It is already preparing to suddenly assume its full rights and shine its light on the whole earth. It contains everything that is necessary for a truly Russian life, in all its relations, from the state to the simple family life, everything is set up, everything is directed, everything is the rightful and true way. To me, the idea of introducing any innovation in Russia, bypassing our Church, without asking her blessing for it, is insane. It is absurd even to graft any European ideas into our thoughts, until it has baptised them with the light of Christ. You will see how suddenly and in your own eyes this will be recognised by all in Russia, both believers and unbelievers, and how suddenly our Church will be recognised by all. It was the will of Providence that an incomprehensible blindness should fall upon the eyes of many. When I look closely at the thread of the events of the world, I see all the wisdom of God, who allowed the temporary separation of the churches, commanding one to stand still and as if away from people, and the other to worry together with people; one to accept no innovations except those introduced by holy men of the best times of Christianity and by the original fathers of the Church; the other to change and apply to all circumstances of the time, the spirit and habits of men, to introduce all innovations made even by vicious unholy bishops; one to die to the world for a time as if to die to the world, the other to take possession of the whole world for a time; one, like humble Mary, laying aside all cares of earthly things, to be placed at the feet of the Lord himself, then to listen to his words better before applying and transmitting them to men."

It was not only Russian thinkers who indulged in romantic dreams of a new foundation for Christianity; in addition to the great systems of German philosophy, various currents of Western thought imagined new horizons for the Gospel message and its philosophical and intellectual elaboration. Recall the criticism of Christianity by the Dane Seren Kierkegaard, who wondered about its mediation of man and history; in the *Final Unscientific Afterword to the Philosophical Crumbs*, he raises the question of what Christianity is, whether it is right or wrong. "The question here is not whether Christianity is right, but what it is. Speculation simply omits this prior agreement, and then claims complete success in introducing mediation. But in fact, even before the introduction of its mediation, this thinking has already mediated everything in the world - in other words, it has turned Christianity into a philosophical doctrine." Thus he does not regard Christianity as some kind of positive doctrine or philosophy. What is it then? It is the antithesis of all speculation, and as such appears as unmediated. Let us also recall Antonio Rosmini's conviction that modern thought in general has lost, in comparison with the classical and medieval tradition, the true meaning of what it means to think, and that in the *New Experience on the Origin of Ideas* he raises the question of the relation between reason and truth.

The criticism of Christianity was carried to extreme conclusions by Feuerbach in The *Essence of Christianity* of 1841, and by Nietzsche's harsh indictment in *Antichrist*, written in the last years of the century. These were the preconditions for the militant atheism of subsequent regimes, and for the great anti-clerical struggle of the dominant ideologies in Europe and throughout the world. Christianity, seen as the decay of the true human spirit, was presented as the true enemy to be destroyed, as an obstacle to moral and intellectual progress and a justification for the repressive regimes of the past. The sharpest challenge was articulated in Friedrich Nietzsche's reflection on the *Birth of Tragedy*, which emerged in the "Wagnerian" phase of the seventies, and was then repeatedly renewed in the following years, up to the cry of the *Merry Science, which* proclaimed "the death of God." In the Nietzschean reading of Greek culture, the victory of Apollonian moralism over Dionysian creativity becomes a fundamental category in the condemnation of Christianity, guilty of appropriating the dictatorship of religious law over the human spirit. The philosopher himself claims that in his criticism of Greek antiquity he pursues precisely this aim: "Perhaps the full depth of this anti-moral inclination can be gauged by the diligent and hostile silence with which Christianity is treated in this book - Christianity as the most unmeasured polyphony of the moral theme that mankind has ever heard...". From the very beginning, essentially and fundamentally, Christianity has been fatigue and disgust - experienced by life from life itself, and only covered up, and hidden, and dressed up by the belief in a 'different' or 'better' life". The overcoming of Christianity, according to Nietzsche, lies in the discovery of the true potentialities of human nature, in that aesthetic epiphany, which will eventually lead to the theory of the Superman: "My instinct, the lawyer of life, turned against morality, then he composed for himself his fundamental counter-teaching, his counter-evaluation of life: purely artistic, anti-Christian. What should we call it? Being a philologist, a man of words, I am not without a certain liberty - for who knows the real name of the Antichrist? - I christened it in the name of a Greek god: I called it Dionysian." In the Dionysian expression of man's will, art is the true scale of his search for realisation and self-consciousness, when, more than ethical and religious answers, man relies rather on the risk of self-transcendence: "the colossal horror that grips man when he suddenly happens to doubt the forms of knowledge of phenomena, because, as it seems to him, the law of sufficient reason begins to undergo an exception in one of its guises. If to the horror we add also the bliss of admiration rising from the innermost foundation of man and even of the whole nature at the sight of the same destruction of the principii individuationis, then by doing so we will look inside the essence of the *Dionysian*, the closest analogy of which is a *hangover.* Then under the influence of narcotic drink, about which all primitive people and nations speak in hymns, then with spring, the mighty proximity of which permeates all nature with its joys, the Dionysian movements of the soul awaken and with their increase the subjective gradually melts, reaching the fullest self-forgetfulness..... There are people who, for lack of experience or out of stupidity, turn away from such phenomena with derision or regret, as if from epidemics, in the consciousness of their own health - thus making it clear that they are 'healthy'; poor people, they have no idea what a dead pallor rests on this 'health' of theirs, how ghostly it looks when the fiery life of the Dionysian madmen whirls past it".

Curiously, just when Nietzsche was proclaiming the superiority of Dionysian ecstasy over the moralistic outcome of Christian Apollonianism, from the seventies of the nineteenth century the first phenomena of Pentecostal charismaticism began to spread in the Anglo-Saxon evangelical milieu, in ecstatic prayers of glossolalia like the "baptism of the Spirit" of Pastor Smith Wigglesworth and others, which transformed Anglican Methodism into a *born again* Christianity that would enjoy success both in the twentieth century and to this day. The Pentecostal charismatic movement established itself not only in the Protestant world, but also in Catholicism itself, almost wanting to restore to religious experience the "Dionysian" beginning admired by Nietzsche. Fyodor Dostoevsky, the writer probably most influenced by Nietzschean reflection, describes in turn a rediscovery of ecstasy in the reverse mysticism of *Besov, a* novel devoted to the nihilists, revolutionaries who saw in annihilation a way to attain God and replace Him with themselves. One of the characters in the story, a member of a terrorist group, explains his revolutionary choice - according to the plan, he was to kill himself to draw suspicion away from the true perpetrators - by an ecstatic experience:

Kirillov woke up and - strangely - spoke much more coherently than he had always spoken; it was obvious that he had been formulating all this for a long time and perhaps had written it down:
- There are seconds, five or six of them at a time, and suddenly you feel the presence of eternal harmony, perfectly achieved. It is not earthly; I do not mean that it is heavenly, but that man in his earthly form cannot endure it. One must change physically or die. This feeling is clear and undeniable. As if you suddenly feel the whole nature and suddenly say: yes, it is true. God, when God created the world, at the end of every day of creation He said, "Yes, this is true, this is good." This is... it's not propitiation, it's just like that, joy. You don't forgive anything because there is nothing to forgive. It's not that you love, oh - it's above love! The worst of it is that it is so terribly clear and such joy. If it is more than five seconds, the soul cannot bear it and must disappear. In these five seconds I live my life and for them I would give my whole life, because it is worthwhile. To endure ten seconds, you have to change physically". Kirillov experiences a kind of incessant rapture, a desire to sacrifice himself entirely to a cause that is not only about changing society, but also about the individual: "All my life I didn't want it to be just words. This is the dream of achieving the absolute expression of nature, of his own self, as he himself states in his dialogue with Verkhovensky, the leader of the group: If there is no god, then I am a god.
- I've never been able to understand this point from you: why are you a god?
- If there is a god, then all will is his, and out of his will I cannot. If not, then all will is mine, and I am bound to declare my will.
- Arbitrariness? Why do we have to?
- Because the whole will has become mine. Does no one on the whole planet, having run out of god and believing in self-will, dare to declare self-will, in the fullest point? It is like a poor man who has received an inheritance and is afraid and dares not approach the sack, thinking he is not strong enough to own it. I want to assert willfulness. Albeit alone, but I will.
- And do it.
- I am obliged to shoot myself, because the fullest point of my willfulness is to kill myself myself.
- You're not the only one who kills himself; there are many suicides.
- With reason. But without any reason, but only for self-will, I alone.
Nihilism. Self-destruction, becomes a reflection of faith and rebirth: a man free of religion must kill God in order to affirm himself, and finds in self-demonisation the true path of deification:
"I am obliged to declare disbelief," Kirillov paced the room. - For me there is no higher idea than the idea that there is no god. For me there is human history. Man

has done nothing but invent a god in order to live without killing himself; (this is exactly the motivation of Nietzsche's Antichrist - ed.); this is the whole of world history up to now. I alone in world history did not want to invent a god for the first time. Let them find out once for all.

"He won't shoot himself," Pyotr Stepanovich was anxious.

- Who's to know? - He was setting fire to it. - It's me and you here; Lipu-tina, is it?

- Everyone will know; everyone will know. Nothing is secret that is not made manifest. Here *He* said.

And he pointed with feverish delight to the image of the Saviour before which the lamp was burning. Pyotr Stepanovich became quite angry.

- So you still believe in *Him,* and you lit a lamp for "just in case"?

The man remained silent.

- You know what, I think you're more of a believer than a pop.

- In who? In *Him?... I don't* understand how an atheist could know that there is no God and not kill himself immediately? To realise that there is no god and not to realise at the same time that you yourself have become a god is absurd, otherwise you will certainly kill yourself. If you realise, you are a king and you will not kill yourself, but will live in the most important glory. But one, the one who is the first, must kill himself without fail, otherwise who will start and prove it? It is I who will kill myself myself without fail, to begin and prove. I am still only a god willy-nilly, and I am unhappy because I am *obliged to* declare my will. Everyone is unhappy because everyone is afraid to declare his will. That is why man has been so miserable and poor up to now, because he has been afraid to declare the most important point of wilfulness and has been wilful from the edge, like a schoolboy. I am terribly unhappy because I am terribly afraid. Fear is the curse of man. But I will declare my wilfulness, I am obliged to believe that I do not believe. I will begin, and I will end, and I will open the door. And I will save. This alone will save all men and in the next generation will rebirth them physically; for in the present physical form, as far as I thought, it is impossible for a man to be without the former god in any way. I have been searching for the attribute of my deity for three years, and I have found it: the attribute of my deity is Willfulness! This is all I can do in the main point to show my disobedience and my new fearful freedom. For it is very fearful. I kill myself in order to show my disobedience and my new fearful freedom."

In the ecstasy of the revolutionary, the great Russian writer prophetically anticipates all the horrors of the twentieth century, the Russian Revolution, fascism, Nazism, and the delirium of the omnipotence of modern man, now exposed by the fragility of his own achievements, of that nameless and technocratic power that causes the generations of the *millennium* a blind and uncertain rage, a need for rebirth to which no answer can be found. This is Nietzsche's own delusion, which ends its existence in madness, which is the extreme and logical consequence of his thirst for philosophical liberation.

Once again, Russian thinkers, as had happened earlier with Schelling and Hegel, set themselves the task of answering and overcoming Nietzsche and nihilism. The Western path led its apocalyptic trajectory to a revolutionary catastrophe, while the Slavophiles, after a phase of chauvinistic retreat that was not alien to Dostoevsky himself (and which strongly resembles the pretensions of Putin's Russia today), tried to arrive at a higher synthesis, a universal Christian philosophy. The unheard prophet of the new revelation was the mystic and philosopher Vladimir Soloviev, who died in the summer of 1900, a month before Nietzsche. In his 1899 essay *The Idea of the Superman*, Soloviev bitterly notes that Nietzsche had become a "fashionable writer" in Russia, as had happened more than half a century before with Hegel; however, "before, such fascinations were replaced rather quickly" while at the end of the century, the philosopher notes the desire to " reach the same mental station." "Of these three ideas associated with three big names (Karl Marx, Leo Tolstoy, Friedrich Nietzsche)", the third one seems to Soloviev the most interesting, "it is connected with what will come forward the day after tomorrow and beyond." Despite the fact that Nietzsche's thought is the path that most quickly "leads to a hopeless abyss," its positive aspect "is striking: contempt for weak and sick humanity, a pagan view of strength and beauty, the assignment to oneself in advance of some exceptional superhuman significance - first, to oneself alone, and then, to oneself collectively, as a chosen minority of the 'best,' i.e., the stronger, more omnipotent, and the better. That is, the stronger, more gifted, powerful, or "lordly" natures, to whom everything is allowed, since their will is the supreme law for others, is the obvious fallacy of Nietzscheanism."But at the same time, the truth is contained in the delusion: 'It is natural for man to want to be better and greater than he is in reality, it is natural for him to gravitate towards the ideal of the superman.', Catching the wind of emerging existentialism, Soloviev insists on the inner intuition of human experience that Nietzsche emphasises, independently of the dispute 'about the metaphysical question of unconditional freedom of choice' that so troubled Leo Tolstoy. It is the question of "the complication and refinement of natural existence, towards that cosmic growth which is particularly pronounced in the development of the organic forms of plant and animal life." In this desire lies the true gift of God, as the Greek philosophers had already guessed; commenting on *Plato's Life Drama,* Soloviev notes that philosophy proper is the expression of man's real desire for the absolute. "The great benefactors of mankind are Prometheus, Demeter, and Dionysus. But the 'thrice greatest' is called and is our father Hermes Trismegistus. In the corporeal image of human dormitory he put his living soul and the life-maker - philosophy - not so that man received eternal truth and bliss as a gift and in a ready-made form, but so that the labour path of man to truth and bliss was protected from both sides - from superstitious demonic awe, and from stupid animal unaccountability". The death of Socrates, with all its drama, gave rise to Platonic idealism: if truth and justice in their most vivid embodiment are destroyed by death, the meaning of life in another ideal world.... It is said that he was nicknamed Plato, i.e. broad (his original name was supposedly Aristocles], for the breadth of his face, and by others for the breadth of his spirit." Thus the meaning of Greek culture was the endeavour to go beyond; Soloviev's Platonism speaks of the urgency of this in new times.

Soloviev's legacy extends to various strands of Russian religious philosophy, from the more "sophiological" Sergei Bulgakov and Pavel Florensky, to the existentialist Nikolai Berdyaev and Semyon Frank, to the more secular and scientistic "cosmism" of Nikolai Fedorov, Vladimir Vernadsky and Konstantin Tsiolkovsky. One of these directions of development most directly linked to revolutionary aspirations was poetic and literary symbolism, whose representatives were such singers of the revolution as Alexander Blok, Andrei Bely and Vladimir Mayakovsky, and whose founding father, who remained isolated from his followers, was Vyacheslav Ivanov. He was a direct disciple of Soloviev, who met him in 1896 and supported his first literary experiments; in the early years of the century, his literary salon was a kind of Petersburg "incubator" of Russian Symbolism, a "creative laboratory" for poets. Ivanov achieved enormous fame in the first decade of the 20th century, becoming one of the main inspirations of the entire *Silver Age,* taking part in numerous publications and literary and cultural endeavours in the capital. The revolutionary storm, which was preceded by a number of peripetias in his personal life, prompted Ivanov to seek ways of escape and deliverance from the destructive madness, as evidenced by *Correspondence from Two Corners*, written in 1920 as a dialogue with Mikhail Gershenzon on the meaning of fate as chance and necessity. While in his most turbulent years [1921-1924] in Baku, he devoted himself to the original Nietzschean theme, writing his doctoral thesis on the cult of Dionysus. Subsequently, the poet, like many other great Russian thinkers, was forced to leave his homeland and migrated to Rome in Italy, where he made his conversion to the Catholic Church [1926] in the footsteps of his teacher Vladimir Soloviev, wishing to unite East and West in his very personality and in belonging to the universal Church.

V. Ivanov devoted himself to the Dionysian theme and the reinterpretation of classical Greek culture in the early years of his literary career, publishing in 1904 the essay "The Hellenic Religion of the Suffering God" and "The Religion of Dionysus" in 1905, and then in 1921 he wrote his dissertation "Dionysus and

Pradionysianism", published in Baku in 1923 under the title "Questions of the Hellenic Cult of Dionysus and the Origin of the Theatre of Tragedy". In 1903 Ivanov also taught a course in Paris on the religious cult of Dionysus. The interest in Hellenic antiquity was motivated by a search for the origins of the symbol in that organic and integral culture which Christianity had managed to assimilate in its own way. Initially, this motivation was linked to internal disputes in literary movements, where Ivanov was the herald of a "new symbolism," synthetic and vernacular, in opposition to the symbolism of the Impressionists and decadence of the late nineteenth century. Art participates in and in some ways directs great social and spiritual transformations: it inspired Blok's and Mayakovsky's commitment to revolution, while Ivanov turned to Solovyov's dream of the religious unity of humanity. All of Ivanov's poetry is based on the Dionysian myth of death and resurrection, where new hope and the glorification of sacrifice are born out of despair, in the optimistic vein of Christian fulfilment and in the indirectness of radical Nietzschean atheistic pessimism. In some ways this theme became the red thread of his thought, that is, the rehabilitation of Dionysism, in a new vision of Christianity. His attempt at synthesis was not easily understood or accepted, even by his correspondents and admirers. In one letter to Shore, the poet-philosopher rejects the attempt "to defend the old me from the new me; this simplistic explanation is essentially wrong. There is a continuous metamorphosis [in the Goethean sense of the word] in my outlook, which makes it impossible for me myself simply to deny any previous moment of integral organic development."

Ivanov's reflections on Hellenic religion are reflected in his collection of lyrics *Nurse Stars,* 1903-1904, which expresses an existential need for insight into nature through myth and the ecstasy of pagan vision. The first poem, entitled *Beauty,* dedicated to the teacher Vladimir Soloviev, mentions the birth of Aphrodite and argues that the goddess herself, born from the foam of the sea, was unable to curb the demons of chaos, and that after her came her successor who perfected the struggle against matter and ugliness, that is, Sophia. This is Soloviev's own vision, unfolded by Ivanov in the Platonic idea of the "convergence" and deep rhythm of beauty and art. The second section of the collection is devoted to Dionysus; as Eridano Bazzarelli states, "already here, there is this mixture between the ambiguous god of Thracian origin and Christ, who would become the centre (or one of the centres) of Ivanov's philosophical investigations; of the two aspects of Dionysus, the joyous and vivid and the masochistic and violent, Ivanov chose the second". The third poem of the section, *To the Unknown God*, (the Christian image of natural revelation, Acts 17:23), insists on finding an unknown god, perhaps Adonis, whose death is mourned and resurrection called for, or perhaps Dionysus, or perhaps Christ. Ultimately, Badzarelli concludes, Ivanov's appeal to ancient myths, his passionate desire to revive them, his desire for panic communication and encounters with the gods ... take on new life and power in his lines." It is a longing for a syncretic Christian aesthetic, classical and at the same time innovative.

The poet-philosopher intends to respond to the dominance of the dry individualism of society entering the new century, atomised and depersonalised, "In order not to be crushed into the dust of dead souls, into the nebula of atoms without an 'I', we must revitalise the individual" on the path of the spirit, the innovative and reformist neohumanism. Ivanov sees at the heart of the crisis of humanism the disagreement that has arisen between "science" and "consciousness," that is, between the objective reality of the rational man and the subjective reality of the spiritual man, a disagreement that leads to the predominance of reason over faith. Ivanov answers this dilemma in the first part of the poem *Man,* entitled *Az ism.* "Azm I am" is the "principium individuationis" of "being." Being knows Himself through Himself." In *Man,* "Azm I Am" realises himself and the limitations that are part of his nature through the Cross, that is, he measures his objective-subjective reality on the basis of that spatio-temporal parameter which, foreshadowed by Descartes, would be explained scientifically in the nineteenth century, but which the ancients had known and used symbolically for centuries. Through the Cross man emerges from the limitations of time and space and enters the divine, becomes a "universal man" capable of perfection. On the Cross is the God-Man; hence the Cross is the form that allows God to realise Himself in the human dimension, so that humanity can return to God and "be" with Him, in an infinite process of transubstantiation between Word and Flesh. The phases of transubstantiation are phases of convergence and ascent, phases of transformation of energy into matter and matter into energy, where each *big-bang* implies the birth of a new universe (expansion) and each universe entails an end and therefore a new *big-bang* and thus the cycle of Life-Death and Death-Rebirth, the incarnation of God and the deification of man. Only in the Christian interpretation of life, death and rebirth comes, in the opinion of
In Ivanov's view, the salvation of man, because Christianity realises itself in the Resurrection: Christianity, compared to other religions, is the most radical affirmation of divine indulgence, even to the point of the burial of the God-man in the bowels of the earth. Any reference to myth contains an independent discourse; moreover, the diversity of mythical elements determines the very diversity of forms in which Ivanov's religious thought is expressed. The factor that distinguishes religion from myth is Faith: indeed, without Faith, Hellenic religion, again proposed by Ivanov, becomes pure mythical symbolism (it *had Gods),* while Christianity, reinforced by Faith, retains intact its significance as a religion (it has

God); Hellenic religion has man-gods, while Christianity has God-Man. Mythical gods are immortal, but if they do not die, they cannot be resurrected: where there is no Faith in death, there can be no Faith in Rebirth. Ivanov uses the Egyptian myth differently because it is a myth of life after death. Life and death are thus respectively the thesis and antithesis of rebirth, that is, of new life. Death does not necessarily correspond to physical death, because the theological meaning of death corresponds to a change of state, that is, one must "die to oneself" (the Augustinian transcende *te ipsum* so dear to Ivanov) in order to synthesise a new dimension of "being" in transcendence. In a 1932 *Letter to himself*, Ivanov appeals to his consciousness for transcendence: 'My connection within me is life, and my life is a connection, I call it in me a soul. How shall I call my connection and life universal? If I am conscious of it as directly as my connection and life, I must also call it soul, the soul of all things. But this universal bond and life is not God, and whoever calls the soul of the world God does not know the soul's longing for God .... *Sacrifizio dell'intelletto* [in Italian - ed.] for me is not faith in God, but faith in the world created by him - in myself. God compels me to say, "I am," and "we are," and "the world is." This is an affirmation of overcoming, at the same time, the pantheism and nihilism of Nietzsche and Soloviev himself: God is not in general "everything", he is the limit of my striving for everything, he is not "nothing", and I cannot destroy him in order to establish my everything in the manner of Dostoevsky*'s Besovs*.

Ancient Greece is not idealised, it is not a paradise, although in the Silver Age its myth and magic could not but arouse artistic and intellectual enthusiasm. For Vyacheslav Ivanov, his followers and opponents, "historical Hellas possessed the looming glamour *of the beginning of everything-,* agriculture, pastoralism, navigation, science, poetry, craft, arts and philosophy." This is a bold and paradoxical viewpoint, renewing the religious search from before biblical Revelation and Church tradition, and is therefore so relevant in times of philosophical and religious relativism like the present. The dream of Vyacheslav Ivanov, and even before Soloviev, to unite "Russia and the Universal Church", to let "the Church breathe with both lungs, Eastern and Western", was overturned by the tragic reality of the twentieth century and the new abysses that were then formed, and before new walls separate the peoples of today's globalised world, we could immerse ourselves once again in archaic myths in order to rediscover the incarnation of the God who suffered, died and rose again for us, who is ready every day to share the destinies of humanity, who is in constant search of His face alive.

Stefano Caprio

St. Petersburg 2015.

## CHAPTER 3

## "MYSTICISM" BETWEEN EUROPE AND ASIA IN RUSSIAN RELIGIOUS AND PHILOSOPHICAL CULTURE

## Speech by Stefano Caprio (Pontifical Oriental Institute) Naples, 3-4 October 2011

### Revival of Russia: returning to the roots

In the third millennium, Russian history is rediscovering itself after such a shocking and contradictory century as the last one. The sudden and to some extent unnatural exit from the Soviet system, which is still in fact the socio-psychological infrastructure of Russian life, has led to a profound identity crisis from which there is still no way out. Comparison with the mirror moral and social crisis of the West, to some extent also connected with the profound changes of the late twentieth century, forces Russia to focus on its identity and history in order not to be drawn into a vortex from which it will not be able to escape.

In this sense, the somewhat artificial activities of cultural exchange between Russia and other European countries, in our case with Italy, are in fact an opportunity that should not be missed, and the task of specialists, in addition to supplying research materials, should be to offer the keys to reading, in order to find in comparison the indications of the future path. In particular, there are favourable conditions for dialogue between Russia and Italy, since Italy is the country that has always been the main element of comparison between Russia and the Western world: a spiritual comparison between the ancient social and religious ideal of Rome and the aspirations of Moscow.

The current dialogue, marked by the uncertainty of the crisis, has made it possible to discover one inescapable need: the need to return to the roots, to embark on the path of recovering true roots. If in Europe there are debates, and sometimes somewhat intrusively, about the need to return to "Christian roots", as an alternative or interpenetration with secular, as well as Greco-Roman or Jewish and even Arab roots, Russia cannot avoid turning to the stages that, beginning with Christian Baptism, led to its inclusion in the great history of European peoples and, consequently, to the acquisition of a far from secondary role in world history.

Turning to the origins of the ethnic and social essence of the Eastern Slavs, we cannot forget that the Russians entered Christian history through the abyss of the religious schism between the Latin West and the Byzantine East, in which they were passive and uninformed bystanders, coming at the most critical moment in the life of the Universal Church, and unable to change its fate. They added to the list of Churches of the first millennium, co-participants in the catholic unity of ancient Christianity, but in fact belong to the subsequent era of divisions, the militant orthodoxy (Slavia Orthodoxa] of a lost Christianity in search of new definitions. This objective historical circumstance has given rise to a sense of the eternal incompleteness of Russian Christianity and its historical mission: the last of the ancient Churches, or the first of the modern ones? The heiress of the original Christianity, or the bearer of a new revelation? To the historical ambiguity is added the geographical ambiguity of the territory, balancing between East and West, between the universal and the private, between the past and the future. Russia will always feel like a "third element" of history, culture and faith: an unintended, inexplicable, superfluous element, yet striking, creative and absolutely necessary. It is no accident that the Russian faith will focus more than any other on the mystery of the Holy Trinity.

The evangelisation of Russia was special, and has few analogies with the conversion of other nations. Whereas the Roman Empire was permeated with the Gospel message through a long historical process, passing through nearly three centuries of persecution and at least one century of coexistence with the social structures of paganism, the barbarian peoples of the Franco-Germanic tribes were able to engage in a sphere largely already shaped by Christianity, which was able to resist the disintegration of the imperial system and the decay of the feudal ages. Charlemagne's policy of unification led only to the completion of the new structure of Europe, which, with the Holy Roman Empire, immediately began to claim rivalry on an equal footing with the Byzantine Empire itself, also in terms of faith and culture. Various Slavic ethnic branches were grafted in at one end or the other of medieval Christianity, but always only as followers of already defined aggregates. Even the great missionary conversions of the new age would proceed in the same vein, acculturating American, African and Asian peoples to the European standards of the colonising countries; and only recently, from the second half of the twentieth century onwards, has the problem of African or Asian 'enculturation' of Christianity been raised as a priority for the young Churches. Russia, on the other hand, was called upon to solve such a modern question by crude medieval means, revealing a potential for remarkable intuition and creativity.

The approximate perception of Byzantine culture, which occurred under conditions of social and political instability, prevented the Slavs, and Russia itself, from taking full advantage of the classical heritage that lay at the heart of Greek Christianity. The emphatically confessional character of the literary culture that developed in the Orthodox Slavic lands, under the influence of the dominance of monastic culture, led to the impossibility of a purely aesthetic (or historical) perception of the classical heritage, in which polytheism played a major role. From this premise follows the absence, both in the Balkans and in Eastern Slavia, of the main channel through which Byzantium continued to turn to classical sources, that school of Hellenistic studies which the Byzantine world throughout the course of its history would never abandon.

In any case, Russia, clearly being the "beloved daughter" of the Byzantine Church, as the Patriarchs of Constantinople like to emphasise, does not simply reproduce the categories of Greek Christianity, and from the very beginning was not limited to the mere assimilation of its content and style, although it is akin to it. Today we can immediately distinguish the Russian Church from the Greek Church by the shape of its domes or the intensity of the colour of its icons, and the eternal tension between the hierarchs of the two Churches underlines, and sometimes quite dramatically, this difference. Russians do not consider themselves children of the Greeks, do not tolerate even the very idea of their historical or cultural dependence on them, and moreover often point out their peculiarity in comparison with the rest of the Orthodox world, and in a tone no less decisive than that of comparison with Latin Christianity, to which they are often attracted due to a number of similar characteristics. The main expression of this special identity will be found in the decisive period of Russian history in the rise of Moscow and its aspiration to be the "Third Rome", the place of eschatological synthesis of all Christian history, but the rudiments of this ideology must be sought in the very roots of the evangelisation of Russia.

Kievan Rus' was immediately conscripted into a religious war, the historical and ideological reasons for which have not been explained, and will not be revealed in Russian religious literature for a long time to come; moreover, it can be argued that the Russian attitude towards Western Christianity will remain rather indifferent at least until the middle of the fifteenth century, until the period after the Council of Florence and the capture of Constantinople. The schism of 1054 itself will not receive an apodictic reception in Russia, which, for example, will be encouraged by the "transfer of the relics" of St Nicholas of Myra to Bari in 1073, which for the Greeks was a very real theft and "irreparable" damage.

The first original "Russian" interpretation of its own role in the history of Christian nations, Metropolitan Hilarion's "Word on Law and Grace," is the first key to understanding the specificity of Russian identity. The role of all salvation history before Christ, Hilarion reminds us, is to prepare for Christian redemption. The law was necessary to overcome idolatry, of which Vladimir himself was a representative: "He alone, who works miracles, established the law, which precedes the truth, and grace, so that human nature might abide in it, departing from polytheism to faith in the one God, so that mankind, as a foul vessel, but washed like water by the law and circumcision, might receive the milk of grace and baptism." The holy theological language used by the author testifies to a deep knowledge of theological sources; the choice of the soteriological diptych "truth and grace" is not only an amplification of rhetoric, but also an accurate indication of true Orthodoxy*, truth* being the focus of the best Russian theology (such as that of P. Florensky), and *grace being* understood as a further expression of God's love, which is revealed in the call to faith of the Russians, a people "superfluous", whose need for the propagation of the Christian religion is not, according to earthly logic, necessary. The Russian ethnos was born on the basis of an ancient universal ecclesiology adapted for a Russia that would have to assume a much broader role than national independence, namely the salvation of the world.

The mission entrusted to the "new people", Hilarion states in his *Word,* is to re-found the history of salvation: "And it was fitting that grace and truth should shine upon the new people. For they do not pour, according to the words of the Lord, the wine of the new, the doctrine of grace "into the old wineskins", which had become dilapidated in Judaism, "otherwise the wineskins burst and the wine flows out" (Matthew 9:17). Having failed to keep the law - the shadow, but having repeatedly worshipped idols, how will they keep the doctrine of grace - the truth? But new doctrine - new bellows, new nations! "And both are kept" (Matthew 9:17). And so it is fulfilled. For the faith of grace spread over the whole earth and reached our people Russian. And the lake of the law dried up. The Gospel spring, having been filled with water and having covered the whole earth, has spilled over to our limits. And now with all Christians and we glorify the Holy Trinity, and Judea is silent". The Russians thus form a people of grace "with all Christians", with whom they are in a state of absolute equality and common, almost synchronous dignity, since the only source of divine mercy knows no temporal sequence. Thus, Vladimir's holiness can be compared to the holiness of the apostles themselves, as evidenced by the significant ecclesiological "list" of the Metropolitan of Kiev, with which the last part of *the Word* opens, specifically intended to offer praise to the prince: "But the Roman country praises with a voice of praise Peter and Paul, by whom they were brought to faith in Jesus Christ, the Son of God; Asia, Ephesus and Patmos praise John the Theologian, India Thomas, Egypt Mark. All countries, towns and peoples honour and glorify each of their teachers, by whom they were taught the Orthodox faith. Let us also praise, in our weakness, even with small praises, the great and honourable deeds of our teacher and mentor, the great prince of our land, Vladimir. In this passage one is struck not so much by the pompous comparison of Vladimir with Peter and Paul as by the absence of any mention of Constantinople and its foundation by St Andrew. If on the one hand one can assume that this is taken for granted, on the other hand one cannot but note that the praise places Vladimir on the level of the Apostles, even before the Emperor Constantine (in turn glorified by the Orthodox Church as esapostolos, "equal to the Apostles"), mentioned below. As for the legend of the founding of the Byzantine capital by the Apostle Andrew, extended to the narrative of his journey to Russia, the Kiev hills, and even to Novgorod, Hilarion certainly must have known it (it is mentioned in the introduction to Nestor's Tale of the Ages), but he does not refer to it, nor does he bother to use it in the Prince's *laudatio* concluding his sermon.

It is no coincidence that it was Russia, at the end of the Middle Ages, that would introduce a completely unconventional element for Orthodox Christianity, namely national autocephaly, proclaimed by Moscow at the end of the sixteenth century. And this is not a detail that can be neglected, but a determining factor in comparing Russia with the rest of the Christian world, outwardly with Byzantium, but in reality with Roman Catholicism. The original Orthodoxy was not at all national, but "ecumenical" and universal, literally "Catholic". The Byzantine patriarchate was not based on ethnic elements, but on traditional and historical ones, occupying the second place in the "pentarchy" of the ancient patriarchs of Rome, Jerusalem, Alexandria and Antioch, i.e. the episcopal thrones that were the protagonists of the evangelisation of the ancient Christian world, the Roman Empire of the East and West, the Syrian and Egyptian world, and parts of the Persian Empire, up to the Indian and East Asian spurs. The consciousness of independence has been present in the Russian soul from the very beginning, from the prophetic anticipation of Metropolitan Hilarion's appointment and from his reflections on the baptism of Russia, and has remained always hidden, coming to the surface only on special occasions. And so it is to this day; tensions between Moscow and Constantinople arise regularly, without ever reaching a real rupture.

## CHAPTER 4

### A long oriental night of Asian soul.

The second stage, which we cannot fail to mention in our search for explanatory elements of the comparison between Russia and the West, is the dramatic medieval passage through the "Tatar yoke", and precisely at a time when Latin Europe was reviving after dark centuries of barbarian kingdoms and feudal oppression. After two hundred and fifty years of "newly converted" Christianity, lived very creatively and with a special capacity for exploring communal and individual forms of life, Kievan Rus faded away, and was cut out of world history by the invasion of the Tartars who came from Mongolia, remaining something of a legend, an oniric country submerged in the dark waters of the lake of original memories. Indeed, such a legend would appear several centuries later, in the context of another difficult episode in Russian history, the schism: the *Tale of the Invisible City of Kitezh.* The sixteenth-century Tale of Kitezh tells the story of Prince George of Vladimir, a saintly martyr, a sufferer of the battle against Khan

Batyi, who will be killed by the Mongols in Kitezh (supposedly located between Ryazan and Vladimir, which the Mongols stormed in 1239, although there is no historical evidence of this). After the battle the body of the prince was taken away to be buried in the Assumption Cathedral in Vladimir, and the city itself disappears, and according to the Chronicle "will reappear at the second coming of Christ, after the defeat of Antichrist". The apocalyptic receptivity of the Russians, already encouraged by the conversion that took place at the end of the first Christian millennium, receives in this case a tremendous impetus that will remain forever, and still remains one of the main categories that define Russian religiosity, which is incessantly in anticipation of the "end of the world", be it revolution or war of extermination, in imitation of ancient Russia, for whom the world came to an end in 1240.

During the period of Asiatic domination, the religious element in Russia seems to have almost disappeared, or rather was frozen, in the sense that the Tatars did not prevent the Russians from preserving their faith, but deprived them of most of their means by destroying the temples, monasteries and almost the entire Christian civilisation of Kiev. Nevertheless, Russia in this period retains the original Orthodox tradition more or less intact, but in a very truncated form, which will be repeated in other periods of Russian history, periods of cultural and religious solidification. The closest to us and most obvious is the Soviet period, more than seventy years in the twentieth century, which are worth even more than those two hundred and fifty during the Middle Ages. The Soviet authorities persecuted the Church rigidly, which, however, was able to survive under the hood of oppression, frozen in the state in which the revolution caught it. After the year 2000 the Russian Orthodox Church did revive, but in the first years after the fall of communism the only cultural and religious initiative was the systematic reprinting of pre-revolutionary books. The Russian diaspora of the twentieth century did not really have much influence on the internal life of Russia; it should be seen more as a phenomenon of religious life in the West. An illustrative example is the structures of the Moscow Patriarchate in the United Kingdom, headed for many years by Bishop Anthony Surozhsky, known by his English name Anthony Bloom, a spiritual counsellor highly regarded throughout the world and virtually unknown in Russia during Communism. His work began to spread in Russia only in the two-thousand years after his death, while a bishop was sent to England in his place to normalise all that Anthony had created, that is, that effective British version of Russian Orthodoxy. Thus, throughout the world, the experience of Russian exiles in the West of the twentieth century was almost completely erased, and modern Russians, even outside their own country, live according to the religious canons of the early twentieth century.

This is certainly not the place to analyse all the stages of the history of Russian culture. Meanwhile, we can note that the Russian soul and its religiosity are revealed through contrast, they are never unambiguous. It is Byzantium and not Byzantium, establishment but also charisma, grace but also the restoration of the law, Christian grace and at the same time Asiatic ferocity. It is the contrast between suffering and beauty, or beauty born out of suffering, or suffering giving rise to a deeper beauty. This theme is more literary than theological, but we also have a historical example, baptism, which is a profound aesthetic experience (the fruit of the fascination with Constantinople) along with the martyrdom of Boris and Gleb, caused by betrayal and cruelty. From what is Russian Christianity mainly born, from the fascination with the liturgy of Constantinople or from the voluntary martyrdom of Boris and Gleb, the first saints canonised by the Russian Church? In fact, it is born out of the contrast of these two factors or out of their synthesis. We can speak of the contrast between freedom and tradition; martyrdom is a free choice, voluntary suffering is an expression of total freedom, in fact this Asian force that can bear destruction, it is an example of great freedom, the revolution itself is it. But it is also tradition, understood in the sense of the strict obedience of Theodosius of Pechersk with his very detailed order of monastic life, one often sees in Russian religiosity a combination of absolute creativity and the strictest obedience to tradition. It cannot be said that in the Christian West there is no contrast between spirit and establishment, but in Russia it takes on a more acute form. Let us recall the conflict between Metropolitan Philip of Moscow and Tsar Ivan the

Terrible, which ended in the martyrdom of the Metropolitan, who opposed the pseudo-religious ideology of the Tsar. And while the metropolitan is a model of freedom, the tsar resorts to violence to defend religious tradition: a stunning reversal of roles. Another episode, the schism of the middle of the seventeenth century: the *Protopope* Avvakum, a model of schismatics, defends the Russian people's faith against Patriarch Nikon, who imposes a liturgical reform to restore Greek tradition, Greek beauty, and for this purpose resorts to the violence of dictatorship and the abuse of the Tsar's state power. Avvakum defends the popular and ignorant tradition of Orthodoxy, where the sign of the cross is made with two fingers, and becomes a martyr for freedom. To some extent we can also think of Peter the Great, an extreme Westerner, who established a canon of exceptional beauty, such as the St. Petersburg he built, undoubtedly the most beautiful city in Russia, but this beauty, rigidly imposed from above, was considered alien to the original Russian spirit from the very beginning. Peter had two state theologians, a Philo-Catholic (Stephen Yavorsky) and a Philoprotestant (Theophan Prokopovich), and he would draw on both. Can we say that Peter's religiosity was Philoprotestant? Not only philoprotestant, but also philo-Catholic, it was a combination of both. A few decades after Peter, Catherine II, a German-born czarina, liberates Russian culture and revitalises it, while promoting the preservation of the Jesuit order and the religious revival of Orthodox Russia. "Gendarme of Europe" Nicholas I in the nineteenth century brings order after the liberal period of Alexander I. And what are we to make of the Slavophiles and Westerners, whose side are they on: the side of freedom or tradition? The Slavophiles are traditionalists, but they propose the theory of ecclesiastical *sobornosti* as freedom from all forms of authority, while the Westerners, a paragon of dissent and harbingers of revolution, want to impose a national and rational system on Russia. It is extremely difficult to draw a line between Slavophiles and Westerners, their positions sometimes overlap and mix; to defend Westernism means also to affirm Russia's ability to be a Western country and vice versa. The positions of the two tendencies change in the nineteenth century depending on the decade, on the period. Then come Dostoevsky and Tolstoy, the first is creativity, the second rationality; in the nineteenth century there was Seraphim of Sarov, a saint very charismatic, and in the early twentieth century the figure of St John of Kronstadt, the founder of the Orthodox monarchy, later swept away by the revolution, stands out. We could say that every aspect of Russian religious culture should be considered together with its opposite.

## CHAPTER 5

### The Eschatological Mysticism of the Third Rome.

Another decisive event, which, in my opinion, forms the true centre of gravity of the entire cultural history of Russia, is the arrival of Moscow to replace Byzantium as the heart of Orthodox Christianity in the late Middle Ages. As is well known, Constantinople fell in 1453; before that, in 1439, the Council of Florence, the Uniate Council, was held, in which two Russian bishops took part. Their fates are eloquent: Metropolitan Isidore, after his exile from Russia, devoted himself to the propaganda of the Unia in western Russia. Abrahamius, who left in his memoirs an enthusiastic description of the Florentine revival, would turn from an unknown Suzdal bishop into a prototype of a Russian patriarchal figure. Thus, on the one hand we see the Uniate line; on the other hand, the direction of Russian autocephaly will be established in Moscow, also because the influence of the Patriarch of Constantinople, who was to appoint the metropolitans of Kiev, will be weakened more and more by the Ottoman invasion. The Russians are establishing their own autocephaly, which will then turn into full independence.

Moscow's autocephaly gave a decisive impetus to the realisation of another ecclesiological concept, the Uniate one, in the western territories: afraid of Moscow's arbitrary rule, some dioceses of Galicia (Ukraine) proclaimed the Union of Brest in 1598, submitting to the authority of the Roman Pope and partly fulfilling the old dream of Cardinal Metropolitan Isidore. These two events are thus two sides of the same phenomenon: autocephaly is the solution found by the Russians after a process of self-consciousness initiated by the Council of Florence and the fall of Constantinople, while Unia is the result, present also in the Russian self-consciousness, of a desire to enter the Western world. The Unia would later be adopted in other territories: by Hungarians, Slovaks, Romanians, Bulgarians, Serbs, and even in Greece. In these subsequent Unias the propaganda of the concluded union was sometimes somewhat artificial, while true Uniatism, as the original concept, found its effective expression in the Russian world as some variant of the idea of Moscow-Third Rome, regarded not as the predominance of Moscow over Rome, but as some form of subordination of Moscow-Kiev to Rome. Be that as it may, both variants, in my opinion, should be considered together, in their unity and opposites.

In 1453 the fall of Constantinople takes place, Russia perceives this as a signal that the historical moment has come for the realisation of its historical destiny. Indeed, the so-called "Moscow-Third Rome" doctrine began to spread at the end of the fifteenth century with the famous message of Hegumen Philotheus of Pskov to Deacon Munechin. The expression Moscow-Third Rome seems to be the ideological basis of Russian nationalism; in fact, Averintsev proves that it is here that Russian christianitas finds its final form. According to Averintsev, the idea of a "third reality" was a global and ancient ideal that preceded Christianity itself; Rome itself was the "third Troy." According to the narrative of the Iliad, to which Virgil then turned, Aeneas fled Troy with Hector's sword, founded first the kingdom of Alba Longa and then Rome itself. Or one could apply this concept to the fate of Constantinople, substituting Alba Longa, then the "third Troy" would be Constantine's new capital itself. Troy was a kingdom that united Asia and Europe, Greece with Asian territories. Troy was an empire connecting worlds, Rome was an empire connecting worlds. There is also a version that includes Alexandria of Egypt and the "ecumenical" ideal of the Macedonian Empire.

Rising from ancient models, the Rome-Constantinople-Moscow direction again expresses the ideal of an empire uniting the worlds; in the sixteenth century, Moscow turns out to be the only bicontinental Christian empire free from oppression. In 1453, among other things, the Roman Church experiences a profound conciliarist crisis: Florence came after a series of conflicts between popes and anti-popes, at a moment of division in Europe, and indeed fifty years later there will be Luther's schism. In addition, Rome was considered heretical, and Constantinople had fallen. Thus the idea of Moscow-Third Rome is much deeper and wider than the simple ideal of national pride. The gloomy prophecy that there will be "no fourth Rome" expresses more the anxiety about the possible end of Christianity, and the victory of the Antichrist, than the claim of the Russians to obtain the exclusive right to Christian rule in the world. This is the ideal of salvific universalism, not exclusive nationalism.

In dreams of the "Third Rome" Russia again appears as a "third element", another element in addition in the spiritual dimension, in religious history. If we turn to such categories as East and West, we see that Russia is not only the sum of East and West, but also something that helps us to better understand both East and West. So we can talk about paganism and Christianity, a dichotomy that has persisted throughout the history of Christianity, which has absorbed ancient paganism, reshaped it, and used many of its categories. Russia has done the same, but in some ways it has preserved this coexistence, this double soul. It also contains the dichotomy between Catholicism and Protestantism, or between Catholicism and Orthodoxy, in both cases, Russia offers itself as a third element. For Russia is an Orthodox country, which at the same time has assimilated many of the values of Latin Catholicism, and in its history has somewhat mixed the forms of Catholicism and Protestantism; the whole ecclesiastical dispensation introduced by Peter the Great is a Protestant organisation, the Church subordinate to the State in the Protestant rather than the Orthodox manner, and the doctrine taught was mainly Latin scholasticism, with some Orthodox amendments.

Even at the thematic level, Russian Christianity is born out of the juxtaposition between beauty and suffering, that is, between an absolutely positive element and an absolutely negative element. Here we can quote a passage from one of the major Russian and world novels, Dostoevsky's *The Brothers Karamazov*, a novel that is precisely trinitarian: three brothers, three human and religious types that are always combining, overlapping, mixing the positive elements with the negative. Introducing his characters in the first part of the novel, Dostoevsky immediately includes a reference to Russian religious history, as the third brother, Alyosha, was a novice in a monastery and a disciple of the famous elder Zosima, narrating his life, the writer talks about the monasticism of the elders, which is one of the significant themes of the novel. Dostoevsky writes that the elders and eldership itself "appeared in our Russian monasteries very recently, not even a hundred years, while in the whole Orthodox East, especially in Sinai and on Mount Athos, exist far past a thousand years. It is claimed that there was eldership in Russia in the most ancient times or certainly should have existed, but due to the disasters of Russia, the Tartars, tumults, the interruption of previous relations with the East after the conquest of Constantinople, the establishment of this was forgotten in our country and the elders were cut off. It is this element that makes Russia so "different" in comparison with other countries, this constant alternation of falls and revivals. And the "troubled" time at the beginning of the seventeenth century was the same turning point, the same stoppage that came in the twentieth century with the Soviet Union, and each time Russian religiosity is reborn in a new way.

In that trinitarian scheme, which we have imagined, the third element, i.e. Russia, should be placed at the top, not at the base. Russians themselves know perfectly well the East and the West, but they cannot understand what is Russia, the Holy Russia, which actually refers not to the earthly degree, but beyond any doubt to the heavenly degree, hence the problems arise. By nature every Russian is a mystic, and it does not matter whether he is a Christian or an atheist; perhaps in Russia there have never been atheists, even in the Soviet period of militant atheism, which itself was a kind of mystic ideology. This special condition of Holy Russia is found in the peculiar character of Russian philosophy, the beginning of which is generally believed to have been laid in the nineteenth century by the dispute between the Slavophiles and the Westerners. There is nothing really antagonistic between the two currents. There is one quote by Alexei Khomyakov, the leader of the Slavophiles, which exhausts the debate: "It is impossible to live in Russia, we do not know Russia." Gogol, in turn, writes: "There is little knowledge of Russia among Russians." Only the directions in which these two currents move differ: the Slavophiles want to discover Russia, while the Westerners want to join it to the Western world, but the dispute itself has no real basis. It was indeed difficult for Russia to find traces of Holy Russia in the past, and even more difficult to do so in the nineteenth century; the Slavophiles in this sense are metaphysicians, heirs to the ideology of Moscow-Third Rome. The Third Rome has not really been realised yet; although this idea is the foundation of Russian spirituality, it is the weakest link in the organisation of the Russian state. It requires that the state should have a high spiritual level in order to govern both heavenly and earthly hail, but no Russian ruler has come close to this ideal. The anger of the schismatics is directed rather against Peter than against Patriarch Nikon and his liturgical reform. It was Peter who ruined by his actions the idea of Moscow - the Third Rome. It is interesting to note that Russian monarchists of the twentieth century after communism, in arguments about the way of restoration of the country, argued that the closest to the scheme of Moscow-Third Rome came the last Tsar Nicholas II, even if from the point of view of the general understanding of Russian history Nicholas II seems to be a much weaker figure. The idea of Moscow-Third Rome is the most metaphysical or contemplative of definitions of Russia, as is the idea of Holy Russia itself.

## CHAPTER 6

### The New Rome of St Peter's

Since the first election of Petersburger Vladimir Putin as president in 2000, who was succeeded by his fellow countryman, Dmitry Medvedev, Russia has in some ways entered a new period in its history linked to the city on the Neva, which was the capital of the Russian Empire for two centuries before the centre of power moved to Soviet Moscow. St Petersburgers are fond of repeating that the Baltic city, with its spaces and buildings, is a metaphysical map of the three Romans: the Cathedral of Our Lady of Kazan is an imitation of St Peter's in Rome, the Church of the Saviour on Blood is an imitation of St Basil's in Moscow, Vasilyevsky Island resembles the cape of St Sophia in Constantinople. St Petersburg has no obvious place in the Russian scheme of things; the city is shrouded in a metaphysical fog. Russian writers often address this theme, Dostoevsky, Gogol, Pushkin: none of them gives a positive image of St Petersburg. This city draws you into the slime, into the fog, into the swamp. This city is famous for the fact that the most beautiful places are the ones where you can get lost, and this is a cause for pride for the locals. With its metaphysical nature, its a-topia, St. Petersburg shows the impossibility of connecting east and west.

St Petersburg in the eighteenth century becomes the ideological capital of the new Western Russia, built and decorated by French, Italian and German architects and craftsmen such as Domenico Trezzini, Bartolomeo Rastrelli, Carlo Rossi, Giacomo Quarenghi, August Montferrand and others. This city fascinates because it has much in common with everything, yet remains unique in its own way. It is a kind of new reality, different from the rest of Russia by its special architectural, artistic and cultural concept, designed only for the capital of the new empire. It is a city literally erected on an empty place, in an icy lagoon near the Arctic Polar Circle, its climate terrible. And yet it has emerged with a claim to be not so much the "Third Rome", but in fact, the new Rome, the new city of St Peter. In Russia, there will always be a conflict between Moscow and St Petersburg, the ancient and the new capital, the southern and the northern, as is typical of other countries. The two Russian capitals are ultimately two different versions of the "Third Rome". Immediately after the fall of the communist regime, the rebuilding of Moscow began, which celebrated its 850th anniversary in 1997; since 2000, with the arrival of Putin, all energies have been directed towards St Petersburg, which in turn celebrated its third centenary in 2003. Thus, at the beginning of the post-Soviet era, a dualism emerged once again: the Moscow decade was followed by the St Petersburg decade, but as always with a typical Russian inversion: the nineties were completely open to Western influences, while the 2000s mark a return to a tradition jealously guarded against the same influences. The northern capital inspired many great Russian writers, most of whom saw St Petersburg as a symbol of evil, the centre of sin, while Moscow and the provinces were usually seen as the cradle of Holy Russia, to which one must return and which one must rediscover after every fall. Thus the changes of these years testify to the fact that Russia is once again taking possession of its soul, peering through its contradictions and paradoxes.

## CHAPTER 7

## THE IMAGE OF ROME IN RUSSIAN THOUGHT

Truly many cultural influences constitute the history of Russian thought, and it is not at all easy to propose a list of them which would correspond to the actual degree of their development. Russian culture can be thought of as a form of late Byzantine Christianity, which went through a violent Asian extrapolation to gradually emerge again in European culture, in the Italian Renaissance, in the French Enlightenment, and finally in German Romanticism, after which it plunged into revolutionary ambiguity to face postmodernism today, balancing between national restoration and the dream of a renewed universalism. And yet there is that red thread that unites all these incessant turns, that place of synthesis to which Russia constantly returns as the shore of destiny, the source and outcome of its own history. And this place is precisely the myth or image of Rome. The eternal city, the universal kingdom, but also the centre of spiritual life, and the centre of supreme power rather than earthly power. Rome always appears as the background of every hypostasis of Russian creation, of Kiev as lost antiquity, of Moscow as an apocalyptic Rome called to save the world, of the city of St Peter erected on top of Europe to dominate the new empire of the modern era, of Soviet power liberating the world from fascism and from capitalist oppression. Today's Rome is Russia, humiliated and insulted, seeking its own redemption, and still trying to unite East and West, saving one from fanatical nihilism and the other from relativism leading to self-destruction.

### The Myth of Rome and the Philosophy of History

The myth of Rome is created in Russia, first of all, as a religious one, having eschatological and soteriological significance, associated with a special interpretation of the Christian tradition, perceived by Russia and repeatedly revised by it, which is clearly written by the philosopher Nikolai Berdyaev in his monograph *The Meaning of History:* "In Christianity there is a meeting and connection of the two great streams of world history and at the same time one of the central and main themes of world history is put and solved in a new way: the theme of East and West. Christianity is the meeting and joining of Eastern and Western spiritual historical forces. Without this connection Christianity is unthinkable. It is the only world religion, which, having its immediate cradle in the East, is, first of all, the religion of the West, reflecting in itself all the features of the West.... By the East I do not mean Russia, because Russia is not pure East, but a peculiar combination of the East and the West. This creates all the complexity of its historical destiny, but at the same time it gives Russian historical destiny a different character than the non-Christian destiny of the peoples of the East".

The fall of Rome, the collapse of the ancient world, the event of Rome, unique in history, was redeemed by Christianity and left the desire to recreate this event, this immanent synthesis of history. This is the tension of the entire medieval *christianitas*, which culminates in the rediscovery of the ancient world in the Renaissance. Russia was not given to experience the joy of this rediscovery of memory; it is achieved by the Renaissance at the moment of the fall of the Eastern world, the Rome of the East. Therefore, Berdyaev reminds us, "We created out of grief and suffering; our great literature was based on great sorrow, thirst for atonement for the sins of the world and salvation. We have never had the joy of excessive creativity. Remember Gogol and the whole character of his work. It is a sorrowful and agonising creative destiny. The same is the fate of the two greatest Russian geniuses, Tolstoy and Dostoevsky. Their whole oeuvre is neither humanistic nor Renaissance. The whole character of Russian thought, Russian philosophy, Russian moral character and Russian state destiny carries in itself something painful, opposite to the joyful spirit of the Renaissance and humanism .... This is the extreme paradoxicality of our destiny and some peculiarity of our nature. It is given to us to reveal, perhaps more acutely than to the peoples of Europe, the contradiction and unsatisfactoriness of middle humanism ... These features of the Russian East denote its peculiar mission in cognising the end of the Renaissance and the end of humanism. It is to Russia that something is given here to discover and open up, and it is in Russia that some particularly acute thought about the final historical destinies is expressed. It is not by chance that at the summits of Russian religious philosophy thought has always been turned to the Apocalypse"[6] .

## Origins of Russia: the disappearance of antiquity

The Kievan principality appears in the middle of the 10th century as a certain agglomerate of tribal settlements with two dominant urban centres (Kiev and Novgorod), controlling in the north and south the trade route "from the Varangians to the Greeks". The historical direction of economic and political development is in the direction of Constantinople, but there are also attempts at penetration from the west, where the Germanic Empire is trying to establish European cultural and political continuity, and the danger of invasion from the east, from where various Asian tribes alternately exert pressure. These three alternatives, Byzantium, Europe and Asia,

[6] BERDYAYEV Nikolai, *The End of the Renaissance and the Crisis of Humanism,* Moscow 2000, p. 122.

would determine the birth of the new state and the formation of its complex identity, also in the following centuries. The Varangian and Russian princes, still uncertain about their nature and their destiny, were inevitably attracted by the power and grandeur of the Byzantine Empire, which had already extended its influence over the Slavic peoples thanks to the mission of Cyril and Methodius, and, after the divisions that followed, gained control over the Balkans and the southern Slavs. Under the irrepressible leadership of the Macedonian emperors, Byzantium in the 10th century becomes "a veritable universal empire whose influence and whose ambitions extend to almost the entire civilised world"[7] . The Arab conquest effectively called into question the true foundations of the empire, taking from it the entire Mediterranean basin, which had been the cradle of Greek, Roman and Christian civilisation. The sudden and complete invasion of the Mohammedan hordes in the seventh century was for the Eastern Roman Empire an event similar to the barbarian invasion of the West in the fifth century, and it was only by a policy of expansion in the Balkans, Southern Italy, and the Slavic countries that it was possible to partially compensate for this reduction of the empire to a besieged province and to reassert the universal claims of Constantinople. In the intrigues of the imperial and patriarchal court, the confrontation with the Roman papacy was sometimes used as an argument for climbing the palace ladder of power, this also applies to missionary conquests in the Slavic territories; in such an atmosphere, the Christianisation of the Russians would take place, and in the middle of the 11th century there would be a final break with Rome because of the ambitions of Patriarch Michael Kerularius.

Thus, the Russians enter Christian history through the abyss of schism, observing it passively and unconsciously, at the most critical moment in the life of the universal Church, without being able to change its fate. They add to the list of Churches of the first millennium, joining the catholic unity of ancient Christianity, but in fact they belong to the subsequent era of disunity and militant Orthodoxy *(Slavia Orthodoxa]* of a confused Christianity in search of new definitions. This objective historical circumstance is the origin of the sense of eternal incompleteness of Russian Christianity and its historical mission: the last of the ancient Churches or the first of the modern ones? Inheritor of the original Christianity or bearer of a new revelation? The historical duality is added to the geographical duality of the territory, balancing between East and West, between the universal and the particular, between the past and the future. Russia will always feel like a "third element" of history, culture and faith: an element unexpected, inexpressible, superfluous, but also surprising, creative and absolutely necessary. It is not by chance that the Russian faith will focus more than any

[7] DIEHL Charles, *Storia deU'impero bizantino,* Roma 1977, p. 62.

other on the mystery of the Holy Trinity.

Be that as it may, Russia, being the "beloved daughter" of the Byzantine Church, as the patriarchs of Constantinople are fond of emphasising, is not engaged in a mere reproduction of the categories of Greek Christianity, and from the very beginning has not been confined to the mere assimilation of its provisions and style, although it is similar to it. By the shape of the domes and the colour saturation of the icons we today immediately distinguish the Russian Church from the Greek, and the eternal tension between the hierarchs of the two Churches underlines and sometimes dramatises this difference. Russians do not feel that they are the children of the Greeks, and often emphasise their singularity in relation to the rest of the Orthodox world no less strongly than when compared to Latin Christianity, which sometimes attracts them by a number of similar characteristics. The main expression of this special identity will be revealed at a crucial moment in Russian history with the rise of Moscow, in its aspiration to become the "Third Rome", the place of eschatological synthesis of all Christian history, but the origin of this ideology must be sought in the very roots of the evangelisation of Russia.

## Prince's choice between orthodoxy and ecumenicity

According to Chronicles, Prince Vladimir came to the decision to be baptised as a result of military events and political expediency. The newly baptised is offered a specially composed and dogmatically detailed Creed, which is an expression of "militant Orthodoxy", waging constant war against heretics; in addition to the details of the Trinitarian and Christological dogma, seven ecumenical councils of the holy theological period are listed with the relevant definitions, the number of bishops who participated and the list of those who were anathematised. In particular, Vladimir was warned about the errors of the Catholics, which, however, did not concern dogmas, but the performance of divine service: "Do not accept the doctrine of the Latins - their doctrine is distorted: entering the church, do not bow before the icons, but, standing, bow, and, having bowed, write the cross on the ground and kiss it, and standing up, stand on it with their feet - so that lying down they kiss it, and standing up - trample on it. This was not taught by the Apostles; the Apostles taught to kiss the cross and to honour icons". In this injunction is seen the distance between the holy theology, raised as a formal banner, but completely abstract and far removed from the practice of faith, and the later Byzantine monastic tradition, centred on ceremonial minutiae and on the materiality of objects of worship. The polemic against the Latins, generated by the difference in ritual sensitivity, culminates in other reproaches equally unexpected, such as the fact that among Catholics "some priests serve while married to only one wife, and others while married up to seven times," and that during Mass "they also forgive sins for offerings." actually ignoring all the classical causes of theological and ecclesiastical polemics *(Filioque,* Eucharistic prayer, unleavened bread, purgatory, priestly celibacy), which before and after Vladimir's baptism would be incessantly discussed in Byzantine treatises on the subject. Thus, Russia was conscripted into a religious war, the historical and ideological reasons for which are not explained, and for a long time would not be addressed in Russian religious literature; moreover, it can be said that Russians would remain rather indifferent with regard to Western Christianity at least until the middle of the fifteenth century, until the period after the Council of Florence and the capture of Constantinople. The schism of 1054 itself would not be accepted apodictically in Russia, which, for example, would be encouraged by the "transfer of relics" of St Nicholas of Myra of Lycia to Bari in 1073, considered by the Greeks to be outright theft and a mortal offence. The annals tell about Vladimir's death in 1015, glorifying him as "the new Constantine of great Rome".

## A New Beginning for Christian History

Another important document that helps us to understand the significance of the baptism of Russia and the spirit of early Russian Christianity in general is the *Word on Law and Grace* by Metropolitan Hilarion of Kiev, written around the middle of the eleventh century. His *Word* is a panegyric to the Baptist Prince, high and refined in its theological content, in which the fundamental thesis that forms the Russian interpretation of the Christian faith is clearly expressed: God's plan for the history of man is the plan of salvation, which reaches its fullness in Russia, called to a special mission in the realisation of this plan itself.

The whole history of salvation before Christ, Hilarion reminds us, is a preparation for Christian redemption. The Law was necessary to overcome idolatry, of which Vladimir himself was a fierce confessor: "He put the Law in preparation for the Truth and Grace - that human nature may be accustomed in it, departing from idolatrous polytheism, to believe in one God; that, as a defiled vessel, mankind, washed by water, law and circumcision, may receive the milk of Grace and Baptism". The sacred theological language used by the author testifies to a profound knowledge of theological sources; the choice of the soteriological diptych "truth and grace" is not just a rhetorical amplification of speech, but a precise indication of true Orthodoxy, *a truth* on which the best representatives of Russian theology (such as P. Florensky) would focus, and *grace,* understood as that inner expression of God's love, which is revealed in the call to faith of the Russians, a people "superfluous", unnecessary according to the earthly logic of the spread of the Christian religion, to the faith of God. The Metropolitan then develops the theme of the superiority of Christians over "Jews", giving the text a crudely anti-Semitic tone. There is no doubt that this is a valid argument of the author, and there are no explicit references to a possible anti-Greek interpretation or to an interpretation in the sense of a Russian claim of superiority over other Christians in general, but in any case, the initial theological means of the "Slavophile" development of the theology of history are already suggested.

### Unprecedented ecclesiology: autocephaly

The idea of autocephaly, that is, the idea of independence from the Church of Constantinople, would remain only a short-lived urge in Bulgaria, which soon returned to a common vision of the Orthodox oikoumene. The Russians would return to this idea with vigour in the Middle Ages, with the result that it would later become the key to the whole of modern Orthodox ecclesiology. Today Orthodoxy is a set of autocephalous churches (about fourteen, depending on mutual recognition), headed by "national" patriarchs or archbishops, in which the patriarch of Constantinople plays a rather symbolic and honourable role, in addition to managing a vast world diaspora, completely no longer linked to territorial roots. In fact, the original Orthodoxy is not at all national, but precisely "ecumenical" and universal, "Catholic" in the literal sense of the word. The Byzantine patriarchy was not based on ethnic elements, but on traditional and historical ones, occupying the second place in the "pentarchy" of ancient patriarchs, along with Rome, Jerusalem, Alexandria and Antioch, that is, the episcopal centres that were protagonists of the evangelisation of the ancient Christian world, the Roman Empire of the East and West, as well as the Syrian and Egyptian world, parts of the Persian Empire as far as the spurs of India and East Asia. The pentarchy was like the five-fingered right hand of God governing the one universal Church gathered for the Eucharist wherever it canonically took place, that is, around any bishop whose apostolic succession was recognised. There was no detailed definition of canonical "territory", much less national ecclesiastical territory, and consequently there was no "ethnic autonomy" in the ancient and saintly Church, much less in the Church proper of Byzantium. Autocephaly was obtained by Moscow between the fifteenth and sixteenth centuries under very special circumstances, at a time when the rest of the Orthodox world was under the rule of the Ottoman Sublime Porte; and even in the Turkish Empire itself, the Orthodox were not considered a separate ethnic group, but an ecumenical aggregate of "Romans", "Romaeans".

Ottoman power recognised the civil and religious jurisdiction of the patriarch of Constantinople over all the Orthodox united in *millet a git,* "the department of the

Romans". The Russian tsar was virtually the only independent Orthodox monarch, and Moscow's autocephaly for centuries was held more by this political situation in Europe than by theological motivations. Yet the consciousness of independence existed in the Russian soul from the very beginning, from the prophetic anticipation of Hilarion's appointment and from his reflections on the baptism of Russia, and remained always latent, revealing itself only in special circumstances.

This mission was entrusted to the "new people", Hilarion states in his *Word, the* mission of re-founding the history of salvation: "And it was fitting that Grace and Truth should shine over the new nations. For they do not, according to the words of the Lord, pour the wine of the new, gracious doctrine into the old wineskins, which have become dilapidated in Judaism: the wineskins burst, and the wine flows out. (Matthew 9, 17). Those who could not hold the shadow of the Law, who have worshipped idols so many times, how will they hold the teaching of true Grace! But new doctrine into new bellows, new nations: and both are saved. And so it is. For the graceful faith has spread over the whole earth and has reached our Russian people. And the legalistic lake has dried up, the evangelical source has filled with waters and the whole earth has covered, and to us has spilled over. In fact, we with all Christians glorify the Holy Trinity, and Judea is silent. The Russians, therefore, form a people of grace together "with all Christians," with whom they are on an absolutely equal footing and share with them an almost synchronised dignity, since the one source of God's mercy knows no temporal dimension. Thus the holiness of Vladimir can be compared to the holiness of the Apostles themselves, as emphasised by the important ecclesiological "list" of the Metropolitan of Kiev, which opens the last part of *the Word, the* part devoted to the praise of the prince: "But the Roman country praises with a voice of praise Peter and Paul, from them they believed in Jesus Christ, the Son of God, Asia and Ephesus, and Patmos - John the Theologian. India to Thomas, Egypt to Mark. All countries, and cities, and peoples honour and glorify each of their teachers who taught them the Orthodox faith. Let us also praise, according to our strength, with small praises, the great and marvellous created, our teacher and mentor, the great prince of our land Vladimir". What is striking in this sequence is not so much the pompous comparison of Vladimir with Peter and Paul as the absence of any mention of Constantinople and its foundation by St Andrew. If, on the one hand, it can be assumed that it is taken for granted, on the other hand, it cannot be overlooked that in this panegyric Vladimir is placed on the level of the apostles, i.e. above the Emperor Constantine (in turn glorified by the Orthodox Church as esapostolos, "equal to the apostles"), which is then mentioned in the text. As for the legend about the foundation of the Byzantine capital by the Apostle Andrew, extended to the narrative of his journey to Russia, to the Kiev hills and even to Novgorod, Hilarion must certainly have known it (it is mentioned in the introduction to the Chronicle of Nestor), but he does not mention it and does not apply it in the Prince's *laudatio*, which concludes his sermon.

## CHAPTER 8

## Universal Russia: Moscow the Third Rome

In the context of the monastic and spiritual revival of the fifteenth century, that is, the emergence from the long night of the Tatar-Mongol yoke, the struggle against the first heretics, the "Judaizers" and "Strygolniks", and the strengthening of ecclesiastical and theological identity, affirmation of the fundamental relationship between Church and State, hence the deep Russian Orthodox consciousness with a rebellious soul, partly heretical and largely monastic, acting as a counterbalance, the idea that Moscow is the "Third Rome" is born. All these elements are concentrated from the end of the fourteenth to the middle of the fifteenth century, and accompany the collapse of the Byzantine Empire. In 1453, the fall of Constantinople takes place; but before that, in 1439, there was the Council of Florence, a Uniate council in which two Russian bishops took part. Their fate speaks volumes: they were the Greek bishop Isidore of Kiev, and one Russian, Abrahamius of Moscow. In Russia, Metropolitan Isidore was an ardent supporter of the Unia, which he solemnly proclaimed during the liturgy in the Kremlin Cathedral, when for the first and only time in the history of the Russian Church he solemnly commemorated the Pope of Rome as his shepherd. Abrahamius, on the other hand, obeys state considerations. He signs the Unia, but then he is stopped by the Grand Duke, who forces him to change his mind. Isidore is first imprisoned and then banished, being sent to the West, where he settles in the Greek Catholic Kryptoferratic Monastery, near Rome, and becomes a cardinal together with another Uniate Orthodox bishop, Vissarion of Nicaea. Isidore would devote himself to promoting the Unia in the territories of western Russia, i.e. Ukraine, where in 1596 the Florentine Unia would be approved in Brest by the "Metropolis of Kiev, Galicia and All Russia". Thus on the one hand we see the Uniate direction, while in Moscow the line of Russian autocephaly will be established, also because the influence of the Patriarch of Constantinople, who was to appoint the metropolitans of Kiev, is weakening and weakening because of the Ottoman invasion. The Russians themselves establish their autocephaly, which is then transformed into complete independence. Since 1453 the fall of Constantinople takes place, and in Russia this is taken as a sign that the hour has passed for the realisation of its own historical destiny. In fact, the so-called "Moscow-Third Rome" theory begins to spread at the end of the fifteenth century, and will find its unequivocal expression in the message of the hegumen of Pskov Philotheus to the clerk Munekhin, secretary at the Moscow court, at the end of the fifteenth century (+1542), which will go round the whole of Russia, expressing the impression widespread, above all in the monastic communities that "the first Rome has fallen, the second too, and there will be no fourth", that is, the third is final. This expression "Moscow is the Third Rome" seems to be the ideological basis of Russian nationalism; but in fact Averintsev proves that it is here that Russian christianitas is definitively formed. According to Averintsev[8] , the idea of the "third reality" was an ancient and global ideal that preceded Christianity itself; Rome itself was already the "third Troy." According to the narrative of the Iliad, to which Virgil then turned, Aeneas fled Troy with Hector's sword, founded first the kingdom of Alba Longa and then Rome itself. Or one could apply this concept to the fate of Constantinople, substituting Alba Longa, then the "third Troy" would be Constantine's new capital itself. Troy was a kingdom that united Asia and Europe, Greece with Asian territories. Troy was an empire connecting worlds, Rome was an empire connecting worlds. There is also a version that includes Alexandria of Egypt and the "ecumenical" ideal of the Macedonian empire.

The last decisive element, which is the completion of this phase after the epistle of Philotheos, finds its expression in the reign of Ivan IV the Terrible. In this period the power of the Tsar was put at the service of the messianism of Russia, an original element of Russian religious culture since the time of Hilarion*'s Word*, which is perceived as the "special grace" of Russia as the Third Rome, as the nation that will save the world. This theme will forever remain in the Russian consciousness. Vladimir Soloviev will also return to it in his *Legend of the Antichrist.* Ivan the Terrible is a monarch who strengthens the state and organises the Stoglava Council of 1552, but above all, he proclaims himself Caesar, *Tsar*, and lays the foundations for the proclamation of the patriarchate by subjugating Metropolitan Philip of Moscow, who resisted his arbitrary rule. Ivan the Terrible defeats the Tatars, capturing Kazan and Astrakhan. Russia recovers for the humiliation of the Tatar-Mongol yoke by going for the conquest of the east, which expresses the ability of the Russians to conquer the world, to acquire a world scale. There are also modern parallels with the conquest of the American frontiers. In Surikov's painting "The Conquest of Siberia by Yermak", the natives of Siberia are represented as Indians of America: Russians with guns, and they with bows and arrows, a kind of Russian "far west", only turned to the east. We Italians, like all Western Europeans, have grown up with the myth of the Wild West, but in some ways we have to admit that the Western was actually already invented by the Russians; today it is the ideological stratum that allows America and the West to feel entitled to spread their model in the world, but the same mentality lived in the Russians who took on the task of civilising Asia.

The Union of Florence was also the destination of the medieval reform of the papacy, which began with the Gregorian reform, the aim of which was to raise the pope

[8] See Sergei AVERINTSEV, *Another Rome,* Moscow 2005, pp. 332-333.

above all authority, ecclesiastical and civil. This process is accomplished only in Florence, after a long "struggle for investiture" and a period of oscillation between the papacy and the conciliarist movement, the fourteenth century with the Avignon captivity, and numerous antipopes, and a whole series of tensions in the Catholic Church. Florence is the conclusion of the Basilean Council, later moved to Ferrara and concluded in Florence. It began as a "conciliarist" council, and was intended to assert the supremacy of the council over the pope, overcoming the schism of the three antipopes. Pope Eugenius IV formally accepted the conciliarist provisions, but then he managed to weaken them by leaving the most radical representatives of this trend in Basilea, and in Ferrara he was able to return the conciliarist deviation to a much more "papist" direction. The alliance with the Orthodox from the pope's point of view was motivated less by an ecumenical desire than by a desire to assert the pope's ability to unite the whole of Christendom, in some way re-subordinating the Eastern Orthodox to papal primacy. Unlike the Second Council of Lyons in 1274 (another uniate council), the Council of Florence was properly prepared. It discussed all the arguments dividing the two Churches, bringing together the best Catholic theologians with the vast majority of Orthodox bishops along with Joseph, Patriarch of Constantinople, the only Eastern patriarch at the time. The only issue left without explicit discussion was the Roman primacy, which the pope intended to be resolved by the Unia itself, signed by all, first the Armenians and then the Greeks, including the two Russians. In the middle of the fifteenth century the papacy had achieved its goal and had in some ways become no longer some dynamic centre of ideal ecclesiastical status, but from some point of view an earthly kingdom like the others, though retaining important theological characteristics. The greatness of the papal court as the highest European authority extends from the fifteenth century to the middle of the sixteenth and it is no coincidence that the Lutheran Reformation would occur in this period because of the worldly excesses of the papacy itself. It is interesting that just at the moment when Moscow feels itself to be the heir of Constantinople and acquires the religious and national consciousness of an independent power, the papacy reaches its highest expression of ecclesiastical and political supremacy; this is one of the paradoxes that express key relationships in history. Thus begins not only a comparison at a distance between Moscow and Rome, but also an ideological and political interchange between the two courts.

## CHAPTER 9

### Monomakh's hat on the Church-State.

The 16th century brings Russia to the reign of Ivan IV the Terrible, which lasted more than fifty years, from 1533 to 1584, and definitively marked the direction of its future development. Ivan became prince at the age of three, after a convulsive phase of succession, and in 1547, at the age of 17, he took matters into his own hands, establishing a veritable dictatorship. During his crowning, the rite of which was prepared by Macarius, Metropolitan of Moscow, for the first time the Prince of Moscow was proclaimed *tsar*, which was the Russian version of "caesar", emperor. The Asiatic headdress, which from the middle of the fourteenth century was given to the princes of Moscow, in all probability a gift from the Tatar Khan Yuri Dolgoruky or Ivan Kalita, is solemnly called the "Cap of Monomakh", thanks to a legend specially compiled in the early sixteenth century, according to which it originally belonged to the Emperor of Constantinople, Constantine IX Monomakh, who in turn gave it to his grandson Vladimir II, Prince of Kiev and grandson of Yaroslav the Wise. Again, the legend of succession linked to the headdress, like the Novgorod "white klobuk", to show the destiny prepared for Russia from ancient times, but actually accepted as a new era opening up for Russia and for humanity. Ivan IV received congratulatory messages from Mary Tudor and Philip II of Spain, who address him as "the Great Emperor".

Ivan the Terrible died in 1584, and in 1586 a new Metropolitan Job was elected during the reign of Tsar Fyodor, Ivan's son from his first marriage, with Boris Godunov as regent. In order to contain the excesses of Ivan's caesarepapism, the Orthodox imperial programme is perfected by the establishment of full ecclesiastical autocephaly. Thus in 1589 the first form of autocephaly in the bosom of Orthodoxy was formally established, the Patriarch of Moscow took the fifth place in the "new pentarchy" of the Eastern Churches, replacing just the Roman throne (which, however, stood in the first place). This effectively transformed the nature of Orthodox ecclesiology from ecumenical to ethnic, and given that the other Orthodox Churches were under the rule of the Ottoman Turks, it is clear why Moscow has since been considered not just one of many national patriarchates, but the Church most representative of the entire Orthodox world.

Moscow autocephaly gave a decisive impetus to the realisation of another ecclesiological concept, the Uniate one, in the western territories: afraid of Moscow's arbitrary rule, some dioceses of Galicia (Ukraine) proclaimed the Union of Brest in 1598, submitting to the authority of the Roman Pope and partly fulfilling the old dream of Cardinal Metropolitan Isidore. These two events are thus two sides of the same phenomenon: autocephaly is a solution found by the Russians after a process of self-awareness initiated by the Council of Florence and the fall of Constantinople, while the Unia is the result of a desire, also present in Russian self-awareness, to enter the Western world. The Unia would later be adopted in other territories: by Hungarians, Slovaks, Romanians, Bulgarians, Serbs, and even in Greece. In these subsequent Unias the propaganda of the concluded union was sometimes somewhat artificial, while true Uniatism, as the original concept, found its effective expression in the Russian world as some variant of the idea of Moscow-Third Rome, regarded not as the predominance of Moscow over Rome, but as some form of subordination of Moscow-Kiev to Rome. Be that as it may, both variants, in my opinion, should be considered together, in their unity and opposition.

## CHAPTER 10

## The Latin soul of modern Russia

Thus the assimilation of the myth of Rome belongs to the ancient and medieval history of Russia and the theological foundations of its image of Church and State, although it was not until the seventeenth century that Latin culture found a way to penetrate deeply into the cultural life of Russia. After the Union of Brest in 1598, the Kiev Theological Academy was established at the beginning of the century, nourished mainly by the theology of the Jesuits, who from the end of the sixteenth century became a strong army of Catholic Counter-Reformation and the new missionary spread of Catholicism. It was during the period of autocephaly and uniatism in Russia and Ukraine that the Jesuits, sent to these lands to oppose the Protestant Reformation, which had almost completely alienated Poland from the Roman papacy, became active. The new Catholic evangelisation took place primarily through school and academic culture and the study of theology based on the Second Thomist scholasticism of the Council of Tridentine, of which Roberto Bellarmino, a Jesuit and the chief theological teacher of all of seventeenth-century Europe, would be the chief exponent. Bellarmino's theology reached Kiev, where it was already taught in Latin, but was translated into Russian and, above all, under Peter Mohyla, Metropolitan of Kiev (1597-1647). He in turn, making great efforts to spread religious culture among his faithful, would write the *Orthodox Confession, a* theological textbook that is nothing but a reworking of Bellarmino, corrected in places to bring it in line with Orthodox theology on the controversial issues of purgatory, the Eucharist, and the papacy, but on the whole very faithful to Jesuit ideas. This text becomes the official textbook of the Kiev Academy, the seat of the entire leadership of the Russian Orthodox Church; in the seventeenth century, Kiev is still a cultural centre undergoing a new period of relative greatness. Ukraine, however, is still today an important source of the spiritual life of Russian Orthodoxy, and the main cradle of priestly vocations. From Kiev came Latin scholasticism, which remained the main method used by Russians in the study of theology until the middle of the nineteenth century. In St Petersburg, Metropolitan Stephen Yavorsky, head of the new ecclesiastical establishment created by Peter the Great in the early eighteenth century, would write the *Stone of Faith, which* remained the official text of Russian theology for over one century, and was in fact a development of the theology of Mogila and Bellarmino. Thus, the roots of the relationship with the West go deep into the Russian soil, even though Russia remains culturally an independent reality, assimilating in its own way also the Western experience.

The real symbol of Peter the Great's reform was undoubtedly the new capital, which by its name alone appealed to the spiritual greatness of Rome as "the city of St Peter", and by its German name *Sankt-Peterburg* declared itself as an emerging European metropolis. The new capital became a model of Western influence on Russia, its "window to Europe".

St Petersburg became the ideological capital of the new Western Russia, built and decorated thanks to French, Italian and German architects such as Domenico Trezzini (1670-1734), Bartolomeo Rastrelli (1700- 1771), C. I. Rossi (1775-1849), Giacomo Quarenghi (1744-1817), August Montferrand (1786- 1858) and others. Yet it emerged with the claim to be not so much the "Third Rome" as actually a new Rome, a new city of St Peter's. Russia's two capitals are ultimately two versions of the "Third Rome." Immediately after the fall of the Communist regime, the reconstruction of Moscow began, which in 1997 celebrated its 850th anniversary; since 2000, with the arrival of Putin, all efforts have been directed towards St Petersburg, which in turn celebrated its third centenary in 2003. Thus, at the beginning of the post-Soviet era, a dualism emerged again: the Moscow decade was followed by the St Petersburg decade, but as always with a typical Russian inversion: the nineties were completely open to Western influences, while the 2000s mark a return to a tradition jealously guarded against the same influences. The northern capital inspired many great Russian writers, who mostly saw St Petersburg as a symbol of evil, the seat of sin, while Moscow and the provinces were usually seen as the cradle of Holy Russia, to which one must return and which one must rediscover after every fall.After the historic victory over Napoleon in 1812, which completely changed the course of relations between Russia and the West, Tsar Alexander I's ecumenical and "trinitarian" idea was to organise Europe by uniting the three Christian empires. The Russian Tsar was to lead this unique union of nations and Churches, and throughout the nineteenth century this romantic dream would be nurtured in various forms, supported by the Pope, who obviously saw the See of Rome at the centre of this union. In fact, in 1848, the year of the irredentist unrest in the European states, Pope Pius IX sent a message to all the Orthodox patriarchs urging them to join the Catholic Church, which would become the head of a truly Christian Europe. The endeavour was not successful, and was rejected without consideration, but it showed how much influence the Russian utopia had on European minds. The ideal of "Holy Russia" was no longer limited to the confines of Muscovy or the mists of St Petersburg, but became a religious myth, walking also in the Christian west. Russian self-consciousness established itself as an integral factor in debates about the fate of world civilisation; it was this qualitative leap that was masterfully demonstrated by Vladimir Soloviev, at the end of the 'golden age' of Russian culture, in his utopian theology of *Russia and the universal church,* where he proposes the idea of a spiritual theocracy as a programme for reforming Europe in accordance with the true Christian spirit, to be implemented under the leadership of the Russian Tsar and the spiritual authority of the Pope of Rome. Soloviev laid the foundations of the so-called "sophiology", the mystical path of the Russian faith, which rediscovers the Orthodox-Catholic dogma in the idea of the God-Man. In many of his works, as in *Russia and the Universal Church,* Soloviev re-proposes his aesthetic perception as the root of a deeper faith, the reunion of all Christians in a single faith accepted in its universal beginnings.

**Conclusion: Rome in the third millennium.**

We have deliberately omitted or only mentioned in passing the influence of the image of Rome on the great Russian culture of the nineteenth and early twentieth centuries, on the one hand so as not to further burden the report, but above all in order to emphasise the main thesis we wish to propose: the image of Rome in Russian thought is not the result of Western influence, but belongs to the original stratum of the religious and civic consciousness of the Russian people. Thus, it is not a question of aesthetic or literary comparison, but of the very reason for the existence of the Russian nation, of its place in history alongside other nations. With all the uncertainty of the new beginning of history, which is symbolised by the advent of the third Christian millennium, the second millennium of Russian history must inevitably resume its path, based on the image of Rome, the universal utopia of the Christian world. And we hope that this utopia will not give rise to new conflicts and new monstrous dictatorships, not only in Russia, but in all countries and at all latitudes.

Printed by Books on Demand GmbH, Norderstedt / Germany